Advocate Marketing

Advocate Marketing

Strategies for Building Buzz, Leveraging Customer Satisfaction, and Creating Relationships

Barbara Thomas, CDM, CeM

To Yesler,

May you always have a bounty of advocates!

B Thomas

Publisher: Paul Boger
Editor-in-Chief: Amy Neidlinger
Executive Editor: Jeanne Levine
Editorial Assistant: Sandy Fugate
Cover Designer: Alan Clements
Managing Editor: Kristy Hart
Senior Project Editor: Betsy Gratner
Copy Editor: Karen Annett
Proofreader: Sarah Kearns
Indexer: WordWise Publishing Services
Senior Compositor: Gloria Schurick
Manufacturing Buyer: Dan Uhrig

© 2016 by Barbara Thomas
Published by Pearson Education, Inc.
Old Tappan, New Jersey 07675

For information about buying this title in bulk quantities, or for special sales
opportunities (which may include electronic versions; custom cover designs; and content
particular to your business, training goals, marketing focus, or branding interests), please
contact our corporate sales department at corpsales@pearsoned.com or (800) 382-3419.

For government sales inquiries, please contact governmentsales@pearsoned.com.

For questions about sales outside the U.S., please contact international@pearsoned.com.

Company and product names mentioned herein are the trademarks or registered
trademarks of their respective owners.

First Printing March 2016

ISBN-10: 0-13-449605-1
ISBN-13: 978-0-13-449605-4

Pearson Education LTD.
Pearson Education Australia PTY, Limited
Pearson Education Singapore, Pte. Ltd.
Pearson Education Asia, Ltd.
Pearson Education Canada, Ltd.
Pearson Educación de Mexico, S.A. de C.V.
Pearson Education—Japan
Pearson Education Malaysia, Pte. Ltd.

Library of Congress Control Number: 2015960644

To Dennis Fahey, my best friend, husband,
and partner.
With all my love and appreciation.

Contents

Foreword

When I think of advocate marketing, I think of Peter Secor.

During my time as CEO of eBillingHub from 2006 to 2010, Peter was one of our customers. To be perfectly honest, at the time I metaphorically referred to him as a "sneezer" (people who *"sneeze" "infect"* lots of others they come into contact with—kind of like going viral without the virus!). Between our company and him, we created a special relationship that played out like this: If we (the company) delivered the goods, he (the customer) would "sneeze" on others in his network. And man, did he have a network!

It turns out that we *did* deliver the goods. And true to his word, Peter "infected" as many folks as he could.

With Peter providing references for other potential customers, giving honest product feedback, having discussions with other peers, speaking at events on our behalf, and much more, we grew from fewer than 10 customers to over 130 in less than two years. Frankly, we had struggled for several years beforehand. In short (and using less virulent nomenclature), Peter was what my colleague and friend Barbara Thomas would call an *advocate*. He became pivotal to our company's burgeoning success—and helped us sell the company at a good profit a few years down the road.

Barbara Thomas (BT, to those of us who have been lucky enough to work closely with her) states early on in her book that advocates are a company's best sales reps, they proactively influence other people's purchase decisions, and they put their reputations on the line for their favorite brands. In retrospect, that's exactly what Peter Secor did for us.

As I immersed myself in BT's book, I thought not only about my own business experiences, having been a serial entrepreneur for the last 30 years at over a dozen companies, but also what I share with my students in my role as a business-to-business marketing professor at the University of Pittsburgh Katz School of Business. Much has changed in the last 10+ years of my teaching there; as I plan for each course, I challenge myself (yet again) to take a bird's-eye view of emerging trends. Of course we entrepreneurs/marketers have all seen a continual evolution in product innovation and development with the advent of lean and agile methods and processes. But perhaps the most profound, sustainable changes have come in the realm of marketing communications. In just a few short years, the marketplace really has revolutionized the entire art and science of what defines marketing communications in the B2B (business-to-business) world. And as difficult as it sometimes seems to keep up, I firmly believe there is a lot of good news in this change.

But what's definitely most important of all has not, in fact, changed at all: great relationships with *all* of your stakeholders. As any one of my students will tell you:

Whether they are created in person, on the phone, online, or through the experience of your products/services themselves—marketing is ultimately all about beginning, nurturing, and developing relationships.

Of course we want to build strong, deep, long-lasting relationships with our customers, but how can we achieve that pinnacle in a predictable, efficient, systematized fashion? And better yet, how can we do that without our direct oversight, control, and intervention? And without devoting hours and hours of our increasingly precious time?

Enter the **advocate**.

Imagine what would happen to your business if you could turn a significant number of customers, stakeholders, friends, associates, colleagues, vendors, and (heck, why not?) even college professors into advocates? As BT expertly illustrates, advocacy is essentially the strongest form of any relationship, and as we engage in it, we simultaneously create ultimate value for our customers and positively distinguish ourselves from our competitors.

You tell me—what's not to like about that?

My definition of marketing is *"reducing barriers to transactions."* My students discover over the semester that transactions are, in fact, a direct measure of the quantity and quality of our relationships. We build trust over time with our stakeholders, and seek to do so rapidly with our prospects in order to convert them into customers. But how do we leverage existing relationships so that we can be more efficient (read: more transactions in less time) in our marketing and sales activities?

By now, you probably already know the answer: Through promoting and rewarding advocacy, we make our customers and other stakeholders stomp and evangelize (and occasionally even defend) our business. As you will see in this book, advocacy not only reduces the barriers to transactions, it also virtually eliminates them. And I'll repeat: It doesn't chew up your time.

So, you may rightly ask, "Why don't companies create advocates all the time?" Well, some do. Mine certainly did, although perhaps more by accident than purposefully. I think many leaders get caught up in their company's day-to-day maëlstrom and don't think about it at all. Some, unfortunately, won't discover the value of advocacy until it's too late. Still others may make an otherwise valiant attempt but simply won't plan in enough detail to make advocacy a successful and sustainable endeavor—less "hit" and more "miss."

Back to the book: For a few dollars and a few hours' time well spent, BT's carefully written manuscript should make an enormous difference in the future of your business endeavors.

With this book as your guide, you can begin today, right now. You can start transforming customers into advocates, reducing or eliminating barriers to transactions, and distancing your offerings and your company from competitors. *Advocate Marketing* will show you the way, whether you are a 1-person start-up, a sophisticated 100-person operation, or a megacorporation. In short, you'll find much in these pages that is thoughtful, relevant, useful, practical, and inherently actionable.

To sum up, in a self-referential or circular kind of way, I guess you could say that I'm an advocate for advocate marketing. Why? Because I've seen it work firsthand, and I'm beginning to believe that it may very well be the most effective tool in the marketing communication arsenal.

That's why this book, *Advocate Marketing: Strategies for Building Buzz, Leveraging Customer Satisfaction, and Creating Relationships*, is so important and timely.

I know that if I had read this book in 2005 (were it available at the time), I could have sold my company for a much higher price. I would have had a lot more Peter Secors and, as a result, a whole lot more Ben Franklins!

Wishing the best to you, your endeavors, and your advocates-to-be.

Greg Coticchia
Pittsburgh

Acknowledgments

I'd like to thank Tony Cornish for giving me the idea to write this book.

I greatly appreciate the assistance and reviews from Alvin Hayes and his support to get this project accomplished.

I'd like to express my sincere thanks to Susan Wilson, Ph.D., who edited and brainstormed with me in the pre-production versions of this book.

About the Author

Barbara Thomas is president of Creative Tactics and is recognized for helping large and small organizations with high-impact, award-winning programs. Known as BT to her associates, she offers the benefit of more than 25 years of experience with corporate and governmental institutions to engage their customers and turn them into advocates. Clients appreciate her clear, direct communication and insight into their business. As a Certified Direct Marketing and Certified eMarketing professional, BT is the recent winner of the 2016 Killer Content award and has served on boards of national marketing organizations, speaks at marketing events, volunteers her time to mentoring, and provides pro bono marketing services to small independent business owners.

She and her husband live in North Potomac with their two dogs, one cat, and thousands of honeybees. BT is an award-winning bee-keeper in the state of Maryland.

Preface

It is in the spirit of learning and teaching that I brought forth this work. As I drive to another meeting to serve as a mentor to protégés from local universities, I think back to those who have influenced me in my career over the years. I have learned so much from my influencers, which include family, friends, coworkers, peers, employers, and world leaders. I'm grateful and appreciative to all their advice, guidance, and inspiration.

Thanks to all the wonderful contributors who shared their knowledge and experience within these pages in our interviews together. You have taught me so much. And I have enjoyed meeting and learning from each one of you.

Now I would like to learn from you, my valued readers. Please share what advocate marketing strategies worked for you and what did not. I hope you will find value in these pages and will be open to trying or applying what you've learned to whatever you do.

Barbara Thomas, CDM, CeM
bt@creativetactics.com
www.creativetactics.com
North Potomac, MD

Part I

Principles and Benefits of Advocate Marketing

How to drive referrals, references, reviews, word-of-mouth recommendations, case studies, testimonials, videos, and more from customers is the essence of this book. The following chapters provide a primer of what advocate marketing is, how to identify your real advocates, why it is important, and what the value might be to you, your company, and your advocates.

As you consider how to apply advocate marketing principles and techniques to help you discover, mobilize, and recognize your best customers (advocates), remember that it is not just about how you can capitalize on those efforts: Help and reward your advocates for being advocates.

1

What Is Advocate Marketing?

You are an advocate. Everyone is an advocate for at least one product or service in this universe. *Advocate marketing*, in simple terms, is the act of asking for action. It is the strategy used by organizations to encourage and engage clients and other stakeholders to publicly express favorable comments about a product or service. There are millions of brands and products available in the marketplace. Some of them make our lives more productive or more enjoyable. Because so many brands impact our lives in every conceivable way, consumers develop a special bond that links them to a product or service they love and rely on. The benefits from that product or service prompt consumers to enthusiastically tell friends, peers, colleagues, and neighbors about how life is better thanks to that favorite brand.

A person can feel very positively about a product, even to the point of believing he cannot live without the product, but that doesn't make that person an advocate. That happens only when that positive experience is shared with others. Therefore, advocate marketing can be defined as activities that identify, access, engage, manage, and analyze results of those customer-sharing moments.

Advocate marketing is not just a buzzword. It has been known in a variety of ways over the years, such as customer marketing, customer success marketing, influencer marketing, advocacy marketing, customer reference marketing, and ambassador marketing. These other names are beginning to converge under the umbrella of a single industry term. For some companies, the function of advocate marketing falls under customer success management, while other companies have placed it under the corporate content marketing team.

No matter where advocate marketing may live within the organization, its recognition by top thought leaders as a critical tool that helps the company meet and sustain its mission marks a growing marketing discipline. Advocate marketing ranks in importance with other customer value strategies such as customer relationship management (CRM), which enables companies to calculate the lifetime value of a customer and leverage the immediacy of the Internet to provide access to consumers across global markets. Advocate marketing's beginnings can likely be traced back to the first word-of-mouth recommendation. More recently, the evolution of social media, including AOL, LinkedIn, Facebook, Twitter, and other communities, has enabled the prevalence and impact of advocate marketing to explode.

The challenge for today's marketers is to identify advocates from their stakeholders and develop strategies to get them engaged in any public endorsement channel possible. Savvy marketers are discovering that they can leverage those relationships to drive their competitive advantages.

What Makes a Successful Advocate Marketing Program?

Organizations need to build and operationalize a portfolio of best practices to create a successful advocate marketing program. Begin by including value drivers, such as recognition, personal causes, and rewards, for your advocates to motivate them and ensuring that your advocate marketing program delivers on those value points. Based on proven value drivers, develop your program with these components:

- **Strategic plan**—Specify the program's objectives and goals, processes, and resources, including employees and budget, technology, and metrics.

- **Program process and policies**—Define recruitment and engagement strategies for the organization, recognition, and rewards for your advocates.

- **Internal team organization**—Identify an executive sponsor and two or more marketing team members who are accountable for specific activities.

- **Technology and tools**—Procure and install software to help grow and manage the program efficiently and communicate with advocates.

- **Key performance metrics**—Identify, capture, and track the data points that will help you measure what you manage to determine the business impact of your program. Track the number of advocates who are engaged; how they are engaged; and how their engagement impacts company revenue, influences search engine optimization (SEO), or expands visibility in the media.

An advocate marketing program should include information from advocate-focused activities that result in customers sharing their feelings publicly. Sharing can be done confidentially, such as in a one-on-one reference call, or publicly on a stage at a televised event.[1] There are a number of ways to promote advocate sharing, including surveys, polls, user groups, customer advisor boards, online communities, product testing programs, guest blogging, recognition programs, references and deal acceleration programs, videos, case studies, testimonials, content amplifiers on social media, press releases, media interviews, analyst interviews, presentations, and other speaking engagement opportunities. An effective advocate marketing program helps advocates find their best channel of engagement, determine compatibility, enable engagement, and strengthen relationships over time.

Who Are Advocates?

Advocates are an organization's or company's customers who then become the company's best sales representatives. Advocates are effective because of their independent third-party validation of your company and credibility. They support and defend their favorite brands—even if those brands are not perfect—because they are relationship- and affinity-driven. Who do you trust more: your friend who recommends a car brand or the car dealership salesperson who needs to make a sales quota?

Advocates proactively influence other people's purchase decisions. How many times have you voluntarily defended Apple versus Microsoft or vanilla versus chocolate? Advocates can be like mother bears—they protect, support, and defend their favorite brands.

Advocates are willing to put their reputations on the line for their favorite brands while forgiving the brand for an occasional sub-par performance. How many times have you gone to Starbucks for your favorite drink even though on your last visit, that drink just did not taste exactly right? Did you drop Starbucks altogether and never go back? If you are a loyal brand customer and forgive that slip, the answer is most likely "no."

Most important, true advocates cannot be bought. They can be encouraged and rewarded in many ways, but a true advocate cannot be bought except through excellent products and services that ensure their loyalty. Certainly some companies deploy gamification programs through which customers earn points and, thus, products and value in their opinions. LinkedIn provides a good example: Members earn influence and prestige through their written contributions, thought leadership, and many connections.

Advocates can be divided into three categories that describe their motivation for brand engagement: earned advocates, owned advocates, and paid advocates. Each category offers unique benefits that can support your advocate marketing goals:

- **Earned advocates**—The most valuable—and scalable— source of advocacy is from actual customers, who are regarded as earned advocates. They are loyal, highly trusted customers you have earned organically by your products and/or services and who will defend and recommend you publicly. The process of earning the devotion and support of advocates is the result of the hard work of providing great products and services that are well supported along with a brand narrative that tells a compelling story. This combination is the foundation for the very best source of marketing—the authentic and voluntary expression of countless pleased and engaged customers.

- **Owned advocates**—These are company employees who are voluntarily involved in advocate programs. Business partners and suppliers can also be owned advocates because they have a stake—and a powerful insider's perspective—in the success of your company. Owned advocacy is particularly important in the middle of the sales funnel, as customers try to ascertain specific product and service details as they get ready to fully engage.

- **Paid advocates**—Paid advocates are **influencers**, not advocates who are paid for their efforts. They include celebrity endorsers, sponsored athletes, and other influencers who are paid to represent the company's point of view. Influencers are particularly effective at aspirational amplification and starting the customer engagement process, even if their motives may be at odds with the company's. What is interesting to see is the rise of astroturfing in today's marketing. According to Wikipedia, *astroturfing* is the practice of masking the sponsors of a message or organization (e.g., political, advertising, religious, or public relations) to make it appear as though it originates from and is supported by grassroots participant(s). On the Internet, astroturfers use software to mask their identity. Sometimes one individual operates over many personas to give the impression of widespread support for their client's agenda. Politicians and celebrities have been known to hire fake supporters, fake fans, or fake paparazzi for events. But this should not be surprising to us. The Bible refers to professional mourners. Even today in some African countries, China, and Middle Eastern countries, it is tradition to hire professional mourners. You can rent mourners for your loved one's funeral.

What Is the Value of an Advocate?

Advocates can provide a wide range of benefits and value. Their value can be measured in several different ways, but revenue is most valued by companies. Citrix's senior manager of Global Reference Programs Lee Rubin reported at a recent event, "In 2014, our reference engagement value programs influenced $500,000,000 in the sales pipeline."

Advocates deliver powerful public endorsements and can strongly influence peers and acquaintances. Through their evidence, other consumers gain independent, firsthand information about how a product or service delivers value by helping clients address critical business challenges. Endorsements can be found in a wide range of forums and in many forms, including product reviews, references and referrals, content syndicators, user group content, market intelligence, speaking engagement presentations, marketing, or customer support content and surveys.

In the April 2014 issue of *Infographic Journal*, writer Irma Wallace described the Statistical Argument for Customer Advocacy. Those metrics underscore the value of advocate marketing as follows:

- 92 percent of customers trust recommendations from people they know.
- Advocates tell twice as many people about their purchases.
- Word-of-mouth recommendations drive 20 to 50 percent of all purchasing decisions.
- Advocates are five times more valuable than average customers because they spend more on products and increase product purchases.
- Customers referred by other customers have a 37 percent higher retention rate.
- Advocates are two to three times more effective than nonadvocates when it comes to persuading others to make purchases.
- A 12 percent increase in advocacy generates a 200 percent increase in revenue growth rate.

What Value Do Advocates Get from Being an Advocate?

Advocates benefit from their advocacy. Even minor acts of kindness provide a feeling of satisfaction. It feeds the soul or makes them feel better about themselves. They know inside that they are helping someone in a way that would improve the life of that stranger, friend, or colleague.

According to Bob Nelson in his book *1001 Ways to Reward Employees*, people are motivated by three drivers to engage: money, recognition, and reward. Because we know advocates cannot be paid, we can conclude that the motivators for an advocate to share their feelings about a product or service will be recognition, reward, or both.

So, what is the benefit to the advocates? Increased visibility within your organization. They gain power and some control. Their importance to you provides them access to your executives. They are seen as thought leaders in the industry because your company is providing their third-party validation. Your organization, in return, becomes an advocate for them. If you are scoring your advocates or identifying advocates, your advocate marketing program allows you to identify which new members would be great new additions to your customer advisory board or other special groups. You can identify those people based on their participation in client-focused activities by their comments about you. As you track clients' activities, you can set up an assessment process that helps you distinguish advocates from other clients. We'll discuss this further in Chapter 3, "The Net Advocate Score: Building on the Net Promoter Score®." Many advocates volunteer to host regional user group meetings, which minimizes your costs. They benefit because they become the big fish in the little pond for the event, gaining some level of control over other participants, who are then psychologically at a disadvantage. Home field advantage can sometimes help their end game as an advocate.

Highlights and Takeaways

The following are a few highlights and takeaways from this chapter:

- Advocate marketing is a proven strategy that leverages customer delight to influence customer buying decisions.
- Engaged advocates are the most effective supporters of a brand or product.

- Advocates are distinct from other customers because they publicly share their feelings about their favorite brands.
- Advocate marketing programs include five components:
  - Strategic plan
  - Program processes and policies
  - Internal team organization
  - Technology and tools
  - Key performance metrics and analytics

Endnote

1. Yes, the act of sharing a confidential reference is considered sharing publicly in the realm of customer reference marketing and advocate marketing.

2

Why Is Advocate Marketing Important?

What value do you place on a customer who provides a favorable reference to a prospect? Would you be interested in a case study that highlights the role of your product or service in a customer's operational excellence achievements? What would it mean to you if a customer shared the benefits of using your product or service on an earnings call? These real-world examples illustrate why advocate marketing should be important to your organization. However, they are just the tip of the iceberg as marketers across the globe have discovered the power of advocate marketing strategies and the benefits they provide to the businesses that adopt them. Whenever possible, bring advocates into your marketing strategy to leverage their power and strengths.

Advocate marketing programs should be a top priority for marketers and their organizations because they deliver huge benefits for relatively modest resource investments. Turning your customers into fans is one of the most underutilized strategies today, despite the fact that new customers referred by advocates are far cheaper, stay with you longer, and spend more with you in the long run. Most marketing teams have little budget to spend on existing customers. In the modern era of revenue marketing, budget expenditures are mainly looked at from a new customer perspective and not for the existing customer base (unless the customer is identified as one of the "dissatisfiers"). Your advocates represent, by far, the greatest opportunity to drive demand and buzz around your products and services.

The biggest challenge is to identify stakeholders who want to engage and share their positive stories about your brand—publicly. Unless they are willing to share publicly, all you have is an anonymous referral rather than an independently validated fanatic who creates content for your organization, amplifies it within his or her communities and networks, and is happy to let you leverage it every way you can.

As reported in 2008, the majority of marketers surveyed invest significant resources to eliminate *dissatisfiers*, the dissatisfied customer who gets attention and support (Figure 2.1). Corporate Executive Board (CEB) experts challenged this practice. Its report shows how progressive marketers have generated greater impact from advocates when they have been empowered—and supported—to have conversations with peers and colleagues about specific products and services. The company shares the challenges and solutions involving advocates for Kodak, Purina, Intuit, Baker Technologies, and Iron Mountain.

How Are B2B Companies Investing in Customer Experience?

What is this graphic? This graphic breaks down B2B companies' strategies for improving the customer experience.

What does it mean for me? While the customer experience is an attractive lever for driving differentiation, the vast majority of marketers focus their efforts—and their investments—on eliminating "dissatisfiers," which rarely sets them apart from competitors.

Composition of Customer-Experience Investments

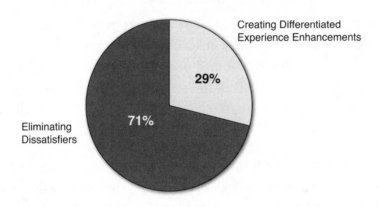

n = 71

Figure 2.1 Business-to-business (B2B) company investments in capturing the customer experience[1] (© 2008 Corporate Executive Board. Used with permission.)

Customer Relationships and the Customer Company Size

When it comes to customer relationships, company size matters. Observations from many of the contributors to this book noted that:

- In smaller companies, customers are more likely to have a personal, highly connected relationship with their sales representative and that sales representatives remain in that role over many years with little turnover.

- In larger companies, customers are more likely to have no personal, highly connected relationship with anyone. If the customer does have a personal relationship with someone at the company, it is most likely someone within the customer success or support team.

Why is this? Because sales teams of larger companies are usually driven to make their numbers and are discouraged from (or not allowed to) cultivating close relationships with customers as they may have in a smaller company. Sales territories often shift and change so representatives remain focused on their quotas to maintain their jobs. Furthermore, budgets are often extremely tight, so face-to-face meetings are rare. Customers criticize that sales representatives only call when they are trying to sell them something. And too many times, they only hear from customer support when responding to an issue they have with the product or service. Through an advocate marketing program, customers who are nurtured feel they are sincerely valued and appreciated, and are willing to develop a personal relationship with the team members of the advocate marketing program. And that advocate marketing team can include staff from various departments within the organization—not just marketing.

Finding the Right Engagement Strategies

A number of engagement strategies have worked for various companies. The strategies have helped make sales teams become successful and, thus, benefit organizations in many ways. This is certainly not an exhaustive list, but it should spur creative thinking of the possible strategies that might fit your organization's needs. In the case studies and best practices captured in this book, you'll learn how companies have leveraged some of these strategies to become successful.

Here is a brief list of strategies that have been used by various organizations:

- Customer references
- Customer reference forums
- Refer a friend
- Online communities
- Social media participation
- Award recognition programs
- Gamification
- Contests
- Co-partnering opportunities
- Word-of-mouth campaigns
- Blogging
- Customer advisory board
- Video participant
- Analyst or media interviews
- Case study participant
- Event or session speaker
- Press release announcement
- Employee/stakeholder participant

What Benefits Does a Successful Advocate Marketing Program Provide?

Creating a new advocate marketing program on a corporate-wide level requires significant planning, cooperation, and buy-in from others, but the benefits are worth the effort:

- Advocates provide *positive relevance* and, thus, firsthand, independent content to any marketing campaign. For example, search engines improve your Web site ranking within their search engine optimization (SEO) algorithm from your advocates' and influencers' content and based on the feedback they leave on social Web sites through blogs, tweets, stories, videos, and so forth. In addition, they are helping you develop new Google Ad Word campaigns, for example. Leverage your customer relationship management data to track and measure your advocates' enthusiasm. Tools such as Marketo, Eloqua, and others can help you score the engagement and participation of your customers.

- Advocates *build your brand.* They not only influence their colleagues and peers, but they also influence the definition of your brand. They articulate better than anyone why they love you and why they can forgive you any shortcomings. Clearly, it is in your company's best interests to engage with them to ensure they maintain a positive view of your brand that they helped to create.

- Advocates help you *secure annual renewals.* Advocate marketing strategies help you identify and assess your promoters. In turn, they help you gain valuable intelligence and insight that helps position your business for the renewal process with that particular customer. By wearing their hearts on their sleeves, they share information that you can leverage.

- Advocates *create the best content.* When advocates share their story in a public forum, they are likely to share that story in other ways, such as videos, speaking events, whitepapers, analyst interviews, and more—as long as they are asked. Further, an advocate's comment in a blog could be leveraged to create a case study, a short video, a webinar, or an analyst interview. Multiple advocate testimonials appearing on a Web site can demonstrate to prospects and customers that you are engaged with your customers.

- Advocates' comments *grow and spread buzz.* One comment from an advocate in social media can lead to her participation on a panel or as a speaker or session copresenter at a global event. As noted previously, social media presence and testimonials influence your company's ranking position in search engines and influence through Klout scores.

- Advocate marketing *deepens connections* with your clients and stakeholders; this helps prevent the loss of an account. By engaging with your advocates, you can meet and engage with additional people within your customers' organizations, thus widening your connections within the organization and helping solidify a stronger relationship so you can promote the value of your offerings more widely. It is essential to connect with as many people as possible within the account because your champion may retire, move to a different department, or leave the company altogether.

- Advocates *engage and get involved.* Who are the members of your customer advisory boards? Who attends your user group meetings religiously? Who is not afraid to tell you what they don't like about you, but yet they still love you? Who do you turn to when speaking opportunities at events and conferences pop up? These advocates give your company the fuel to increase customer engagement and involvement. This adds value, builds buzz, and creates content. It drives leads and generates sales by identifying, assessing, scoring, and engaging those advocates. Engagement and involvement with your customers causes them to speak with one voice on your behalf. Their positive word-of-mouth efforts and online activities increase your relevance to prospects. You may even gain support for a new purchase or renewal.

- Advocate marketing *improves customer satisfaction and delight scoring processes.* This gives you the data points to consolidate and analyze all of your independent surveys, polls, and questionnaires about satisfaction and delight to truly understand the substance and value of your advocates. This translates to smarter marketing and improves your opportunities for greater profits, targeted service delivery, and new products. This also allows you to understand the conflicts or the synergies that are created. You may already have the tools in hand to do this or you may need to supplement with a few tools. A CRM tool and a lead nurturing tool can help support your advocate marketing goals—minus the strategies and expertise.

- Advocate marketing can *improve event and workshop attendance.* Your advocates create buzz, which draws colleagues and peers to your event. They will bring their team members or suggest the event to others. Salesforce.com used this strategy in the early 2000s when the company invited regional customers to speak at its events. The invitees helped draw in local attendance, as well as bring in colleagues and peers from various organizations as attendees. Regional speakers help you expand your reach and improve attendance at events, webinars, and workshops. Their success is your success.

This list illustrates just why advocate marketing should be a component in your overall marketing plan. It should be a key playbook strategy to be built in through all your marketing channels starting with your database tools. You may need to create a business case to persuade stakeholders to get on board with the change to a customer-centric advocate marketing approach if all they have known is a product-centric marketing approach. It is a change in mind-set but one that is very worthy of considering.

Extend and deepen the relationship by listening carefully to what clients are sharing publicly. Pay particular attention to what they value most and how your products and services are making them successful, and incorporate this intelligence into your sales process and training. Look for trends for what advocates are sharing and bolster those areas. For example, if they are sharing how much they value your educational webinars or analytical insights shared in a blog, your company should increase those activities. Likewise, identify areas that customers value least. Consider those areas opportunities for improvement or investment. Product marketing and managers can leverage information obtained from advocates just as much if not more than sales and marketing teams. Smart organizations listen to what their advocates are saying—and pay attention to what they are not saying, too.

Advocate Marketing Program Drives Demand and Buzz and Sales

Momentum is growing to incorporate advocate marketing into corporate America. A clear sign of its growing popularity is the growth of social media in the past two years and the number of articles, videos, blogs, tweets, and e-mails created every 60 seconds online (see Figure 2.2).

Figure 2.2 Explosive growth of Internet transactions[2] (Image courtesy of the Centre for Learning and Teaching, Vocational Training Council, Hong Kong [2014])

People are sharing all aspects of their life and influencing others. The growing market interests have enabled the rise of advocate marketing firms, such as Influitive, GYK Antler, Intel, Reputation Advocate, Inc., and others, that have established themselves as industry leaders by implementing successful advocate marketing tools and programs to both B2B and B2C (business-to-consumer) companies. Their stories are shared within this book.

Highlights and Takeaways

The following are a few highlights and takeaways from this chapter:

- Advocates give you credibility and provide your third-party validation.

- Advocates provide positive relevance.

- Advocates build your brand.

- Advocates help you secure annual renewals.

- Advocates create the best content.

- Advocate marketing deepens connections with your clients and stakeholders.

- Advocates engage and get involved.

- Advocate marketing improves customer satisfaction and delight scoring processes.

- Advocate marketing can improve event and workshop attendance.

Endnotes

1. CEB Research Customer Loyalty graph—https://www.executiveboard.com/member/marketing-midsized/research/general/14/how-are-b2b-companies-investing-in-customer-experience.html?referrerTitle=Loyalty%20%26%20Advocacy%20-%20CEB%20Marketing%20Leadership%20Council%20for%20Midsized%20Companies

2. Center for Learning and Teaching—https://clt.vtc.edu.hk/what-happens-online-in-60-seconds/

3

The Net Advocate Score: Building on the Net Promoter Score®

All organizations seek to grow. Outside of mergers and acquisitions, growth usually occurs when stakeholders enjoy doing business with a company. When engaging with a company is easy and satisfying, they invest in the organization, buy more of its products and services, and share their positive experiences with friends and colleagues. The happier the stakeholder, the more he or she is likely to be a part of that company's community. And when that happiest level of satisfaction is reached, an advocate is created.

Tracking and measuring how a stakeholder feels about a brand or product and establishing accountability for the stakeholder experience has become easier by using sophisticated technology and correlating specific questions with stakeholder behavior.

Several years ago, Fred Reichheld and a team from the management consultancy group Bain & Company conducted research testing a variety of questions. Through their research, they determined that "one question" worked best for determining repurchases, referrals, and a strong sense of advocacy. That was the birth of the Net Promoter Score, or NPS®, question. The simple question is:

What is the likelihood that you would recommend Company X to a friend or colleague?

In my experience, I have found that the "one question" is not always sufficient for identifying advocates. Recall the true definition of an advocate: *a person who publicly supports or recommends a particular cause or policy.*

The "one question" methodology does not capture whether the stakeholder is willing to be public about her satisfaction or happiness. There is no confirmation of commitment to share with friends or colleagues. That is crucial in scoring a stakeholder's value to the company. In order to capture how firm that commitment is, Creative Tactics created the *Net Advocate Score* (NAS) to take into account a stakeholder's commitment for public attribution of positive opinions.

Back in 2006 and 2007 while interviewing and surveying several companies about major efficiency gains and cost savings they had achieved after implementing a client's information management solution, I had an "aha moment" that led to the creation of the Net Advocate Score calculation.

In one interview, a stakeholder provided glowing endorsements about his experience, enthusiastically indicated he planned to recommend the product to his industry peers, and assured me that he would be renewing the annual service contract. However, the stakeholder quickly balked when I asked if the comments could be shared publicly.

"Wait a second," I thought. "This person has a NPS of 9, yet he's tying my hands by not promoting my client in public. That's not the definition of a promoter."

From that point forward, I have made clear distinctions between companies that endorse their suppliers in public and those that only endorse in private. I firmly believe that comments made in private should not be treated equally as those that allow their comments to be published for public viewing, even if the restriction is driven by a legal or compliance mandate. A public endorsement has greater value than one that is delivered in private, and, as such, the NAS score should be adjusted to reflect the difference.

In today's competitive business environment, corporate decision makers research suppliers and products months before a formal sales cycle begins. Getting those public endorsements from advocates significantly influences future buying decisions. Therefore, open expressions of love and satisfaction for a company's brand and services are more valuable to companies than the accolades delivered privately— in most cases. Advocates who choose not to publicly support their favorite brands more closely resemble the definition of a passive or detractor and should be scored as such.

The NAS serves as a more accurate assessment of how well a company meets public esteem and is the cornerstone to a company's strategic marketing plans. The NAS delivers great value by confirming the public engagement of stakeholders and promoting a company's brand and products in a positive, successful, and open forum. The NAS score is not a stakeholder satisfaction score. Rather, it enables organizations to identify their best advocates through a two-question process and allows them to calculate their company NAS with greater accuracy.

A closer look at the NAS process and formulas will illustrate how it provides a strong, quantifiable measure of commitment and, thus, advocacy.

Calculating the Net Advocate Score

The NAS scores divide stakeholders into three distinct categories: advocates, passives, and detractors. Under the NAS methodology, stakeholder responses are scored on any Likert scale (similar to NPS). Using a scale of 0–10, advocates are scored at 9 to 10 points, passives receive 7 or 8 points, and detractors are scored at 6 points or below. But unlike NPS, scoring is calculated using a two-part process, not just one question. Let's look at how Part A and Part B generate a more accurate assessment of advocacy.

Part A: Determine the Likelihood of a Recommendation

Part A introduces the "one question" posed by the NPS. Companies ask their stakeholders,

"What is the likelihood you would recommend [my organization or product] to a friend or colleague?"

Part A: What is the likelihood you would recommend Company X to a friend or colleague?

0	1	2	3	4	5	6	7	8	9	10
Not likely at all					Neutral					Extremely likely

Stakeholders choose a score on an 11-point scale (or any Likert scale you choose). In this example, 10 indicates that the stakeholder is *extremely likely to recommend*, and 0 (zero) indicates that the stakeholder is *not likely at all to recommend*.

Fundamentally, the three categories are defined thus:

- *Advocates* (9–10) are promoters and loyalists, keep buying, refer others, and fuel growth.
- *Passives* (7–8) are satisfied but vulnerable to competitive offerings.
- *Detractors* (0–6) are unhappy, could damage the brand, and inhibit growth.

Once this question is answered, Part B provides the real value in determining which of your stakeholders will provide real, sustainable value as front-line advocates.

Part B: Confirm the Commitment

This step helps to assess and confirm the level of commitment you can expect from the advocate. Part B asks the additional question:

"Can we publicly share your recommendation of us?"

Part B: Can we publicly share your recommendation of us?

NO   YES

–2   0

Stakeholders who choose "YES" keep their original score and are classified as *advocates*. Stakeholders who choose "NO" have 2 points subtracted from their Part A score, dropping them back into the *passive* category.[1] They may say they are extremely likely to recommend but *will not confirm it* with their willingness to announce it publicly. This 2-point subtraction is important to calculate into the results; otherwise, a company can overstate its results, leaving it vulnerable to unspecified risks and overstatements of potential growth. The risk is that the company has a higher level of confidence that an account is not at risk when, in fact, it might be.

Calculating an Organization's NAS

To calculate an organization's NAS score, take the percentage of the stakeholders who are accurately scored as *advocates* and subtract the percentage of stakeholders who are *detractors*. (This is the same process followed for NPS calculations.) The NAS is not expressed as a percentage but as an absolute number between –100 and +100.

Here is an example of the same survey processed using the NAS and NPS methodologies.

NAS Results

Company A performed a survey and received the following scores for stakeholders using the NAS methodology: 25 percent advocates,

55 percent passives, and 20 percent detractors. Subtract the percentage of detractors from the percentage of advocates to determine the NAS:

+25 – 20 = +5 (the company's NAS)

In this example, the company's NAS is 5. Generally, anything above a 0 is considered a good score. This score suggests that steps should be taken to improve customer satisfaction because the score can always be higher. There is always room for improvement.

NPS Results

Company B performed a survey and received the following scores for your stakeholders using the NPS methodology: 35 percent promoters, 45 percent passives, and 20 percent detractors. These numbers are higher because the commitment—the willingness to engage—was not factored in. Subtract the percentage of detractors from the percentage of advocates to determine the NAS:

+35 – 20 = +15 (the company's NPS)

In this example, the company's NPS is 15. This overstated NPS score provides a false sense of confidence, does not identify public commitment, and camouflages growth vulnerabilities and risks. By incorporating the "second question," the NAS becomes the more effective tool for empowering organizations to measure and identify their best stakeholders because it provides a realistic assessment of the likelihood of accurate advocate identification and support.

The NAS score can be used by companies to more accurately identify customer happiness. It gives an organization an easy-to-understand number for all stakeholders and another useful key performance indicator for managers. By tracking the evolution of the NAS over time, companies can correlate the score to revenue growth for benchmarking and evaluation. When more industries adopt the NAS, companies will be able to determine their position versus their peers, competition, and the industry average.

The NAS score is just one key performance indicator (KPI) metric that can be included in customer satisfaction surveys. Other KPIs that can be tracked include determining a satisfaction score, renewal, or repeat purchase probability score and ease-of-doing-business score. Computations of these KPIs are powerful tools that help companies with predictive modeling and business and customer insights. Keep in mind, however, that NPS and NAS scores represent a point in time. A stakeholder can score as an advocate on one survey and score as a detractor on the next survey. There are many contributing factors as to why a stakeholder scores a certain way. Identifying these factors is something a company should do quickly and have the mechanisms in place to make it happen seamlessly and routinely.

One or Two Questions Do Not Constitute an Advocate Marketing Strategy

To understand the motives of an advocate—or for that matter, a detractor—I recommend that you add an open-ended question to surveys that probes the underlying reasons behind the scoring question to recommend. Through qualitative assessment, the company can better understand the motives and value of the score and possibly make further adjustments to the company's overall score.

Effective stakeholder engagement processes can fine-tune a company's growth engine by addressing strategic concerns around identifying, assessing, managing, and analyzing advocate engagement, including:

- Does it promote strategic engagement and efficiency?
- Does it clarify and simplify the process of delighting stakeholders?
- Does it enable assessment and management of stakeholders?

- Does it enable decision makers to compare performance across key time intervals?
- Is there a dashboard for quick, easy evaluations?

Companies that routinely monitor and measure their percentage of advocates can generate key information from stakeholders and drive better decisions. Many times, the improvements that are made help transform passives and detractors into higher-level scores and, thus, advocates.

Highlights and Takeaways

The following are a few highlights and takeaways from this chapter:

- Tracking and measuring how a stakeholder feels about a brand or product and establishing accountability for the stakeholder experience is supported by several models, each with different strengths.
- Unlike other advocate assessment scoring models, the Net Advocate Score (NAS) captures stakeholders' commitment for public attribution of positive opinions.
- The NAS enables organizations to more accurately identify their best advocates through a two-question process, allowing greater accuracy for calculating a company's NAS.
- Subtracting 2 points from the NPS score creates a new, more accurate NAS score by removing stakeholders who do not confirm with public commitment.
- Once an advocate is identified and qualified, quick action is required to get them publicly engaged in a smooth and methodical manner.

- Companies that routinely monitor and measure advocates have solid data from which to make better business decisions.

Endnote

1. Depending on the scale you use, you may need to change the number to subtract. For example, a 0–8 scale may require subtracting just 1 point.

Part II

Case Studies and Best Practices: Words from the Experts

The case studies and best practices included in this section were written by expert contributors in order to share their experiences, great ideas, cautionary tales, and unique perspectives that both include and bound advocate marketing. While they differ in their structure and expression, each brings up points that speak to the variety of business focus, corporate cultures, and organization personalities. Taken together, many common themes become evident, and they provide real-world, tried-and-true instruction in the role and value advocates can bring to any organization.

Each contains a list of highlights that are the key takeaway points. Also, to understand more about the contribution and the starting point for each essay, a brief biography is included. It is clear that these contributors walk the talk by living the role of an advocate.

4

Build an Advocate Recognition Engagement (ARE) Program

In 2006, a midsized company headquartered in Tempe, Arizona, faced the challenge of encouraging more of its customers to share how the company's environmental, health and safety, emergency, and sustainability software and professional services were helping it meet its strategic corporate goals. On average, on an annual basis, between four and eight customers agree to share their success stories publicly in case studies and press releases. In some cases, the company agrees to some financial discount at renewal that would incentivize the customer to participate.[1] In other cases, the product champion agrees to write a case study, but the organization's internal legal counsel or communications executive squashes the client's participation. The company marketers were perplexed. They pondered how to get more case studies from customers, and how to remove barriers erected by legal and communication teams.

As the associate vice president of marketing for the company, this dilemma was indirectly mine. Although it wasn't part of my direct responsibilities, finding a resolution to the challenge would benefit me and my team. While reading *1001 Ways to Reward Employees*[2] by Bob Nelson and Stephen Schudlich, I had one of those "aha" moments. Nelson and Schudlich assert that people are motivated by three basic things: *money, recognition,* and *rewards.* They pointed out that recognition and reward have deeper meaning and stronger influence, and, thus, they resonate with people more. Their theory helped inspire me to develop the Advocate Recognition Engagement

(ARE) program. By publicly recognizing and rewarding customers, they would, in turn, fulfill our need for case studies and other marketing assets. Over the years, the program evolved into so much more.

The Excellence Award program (a part of the ARE program) turned out to be one of the best content development programs for our company. Once implemented, the program was tied to the company biannual user conference. In 2006, the inaugural year for the program, the Excellence Awards delivered 18 case studies, up more than 200 percent over the 8 case studies delivered in 2005. We were thrilled that some of these new contributors had previously declined to participate. In 2008, the company generated 43 customer case studies.

Any inaugural program is tough to get off the ground. It hasn't been done before and people hate change. We launched an internal educational webinar about the program, covering FAQs for them and FAQs to share with their customers. We wanted to get 10 customers to participate. Most of the staff accepted the strategy of the program and supported it. Some people rooted for me to fail and fall on my face. (We all have our haters.) I'm proud to say this program worked and continues to work as other companies have adopted the program.

As it matured, the Excellence Award program answered other important questions for our company, such as:

- How can we increase marketing assets for lead nurturing programs?
- What thought leadership topics should be the focus of our content in the upcoming months?
- What customers can we get to speak with us at upcoming events and webinars?
- Where can the next user group meetings be held on our limited budget?
- How can we get more stakeholders engaged?

After outlining the possible strategies to the chief marketing officer through a detailed business case, we got the green light to move forward with a limited budget. I captured the process and requirements into the six steps discussed in this chapter. They are the cornerstones of the program.

Step One: Identify Customers with Sales and Support Teams

Working with the customer care and sales teams to identify customers who had used the company's solution for more than one year with no reported troubles or open service issue tickets, we developed a list of hundreds of small, medium, and large companies that use our software tools, products, and services. We hoped to encourage a wide variety of customers to share insights. We wanted a diverse pool to consult so we could learn from the perspectives of various industries, company sizes, regional locations, business unit involvement, and more.

Working with our company's internal teams helped announce the program to everyone in each company we explored. We formed a small leadership group with representation from each business line. Employees were directed to their key team member should any questions arise. If they could not address questions, they would turn to me for help.

The Excellence Award program could not succeed in isolation. One top priority was to develop strong collaborative relationships with all customer-facing teams. Communication with all internal stakeholders was key to the program's success. Also, we needed an entry form with rules and guidelines that protected our interests, but did not have the intimidating look of a legal contract. We were able to get our legal counsel to help us get the right phrasing and work with us should anyone want to make edits to it. If the company is big enough and their case study is desired enough, they could force an edit.

Another top priority was infrastructure for the program. My CMO and I worked to build out enough of the infrastructure to get things started. Whatever we didn't have by then, we created it along the way. The key components we started with were a list of all of the roles and responsibilities that would support the program, a creative brief, a budget, a timeline, some goals for number of case studies, an entry form, judging criteria, a FAQ for internal staff that explained the benefits of the program, a FAQ for customers that explained the benefits for them, a FAQ for sponsors, and internal and public Web pages so people could confirm we were real and we were serious about the award program.

Step Two: Create an E-mail and Phone Strategy for Identified Customer Accounts

Using e-mailing best practices, we created a unique e-mail template using insights from Bob Nelson's book. Leveraging the sentiment of recognition and reward, each person received a personal e-mail from a person's real e-mail address with a simple but engaging subject line. To this day, it still has the highest open rate of any e-mail campaign I've ever been involved with—over 90 percent open rate and a double-digit response rate. The subject line continues to have a very high effective rate even today. The e-mail was text format only—simple and direct. We later changed the formatting to HTML to make the e-mails more eye-catching and attractive. We learned, however, that taking a plain approach to creating the e-mail content was more effective in driving interested customers to respond. We had over a hundred inquiries. Our DO NOT EMAIL list did grow, but only by .01 percent of the list size.

As noted earlier, we created FAQ sheets for sales and customer care teams. However, most phone calls were funneled to one person—me. Because the Excellence Award program was so new, everyone wanted to have me join them on calls or handle the customer questions. E-mail responses came directly to me. We followed up with phone calls within two to three days of the e-mail's receipt to assure key account users that we had read their note.

Follow-up e-mails were scheduled five days later. By replying directly to the initial e-mail and including a quick note, we asked whether the customer had seen our previous response and if he had any questions.

Dozens of users responded. There were multiple users from the same companies; this allowed us to coordinate groups from each account to get interviews from different types of users, from system implementers through executive managers. We had scheduled 21 interviews with customers who were interested in winning the award and being part of the award program.

Step Three: Interview and Write Case Study Entries by the User Conference Deadline

Companies that write case studies about the product are doing it wrong. Case studies should be all about the customer being enabled to succeed, and the product is one of the tools it uses to reach that success.

Because customers have full-time jobs and the case study was an important element to their entry, I created a process through which we would interview the customers, create a transcript to work from, and present a draft of their entry to them based on the information they shared during the interview.

Before interviewing the customers, we interviewed our company staffers who knew the customers, their experiences with the product, and successes they experienced. These insights helped us identify which questions should be asked and what phrasing and testimonials were desired.

All customer interviews were recorded and transcribed to make sure that we captured a full set of notes. Those interviews followed a set of protocols and included carefully crafted questions for each product. We created a hybrid of interview questions in advance for specific customers in order to identify their challenges, business strategic goals that were involved with those challenges, and the results they experienced—their metrics of success. Success isn't always measured in time saved or reduced operating costs. In some cases, success can be defined by how the software enhanced the client's management capabilities, increased transparency, improved operational efficiency, or reduced risk. These metrics of success enabled increased sales and created greater value for customers.

Internal interviews should involve a maximum of three customer account stakeholders. Too many internal stakeholders in the conversation may cause conflict without yielding much actionable information. Getting information by committee can be just as hard to do as making a decision by committee—and just as messy.

Customer interviews should always start with introductions. Have everyone on the call state their name, title, and years with the company or other quick pieces of information so that transcribing tools can identify the tone of the speaker and easily transcribe who is speaking as the conversation happens. Try to give everyone who was on the call a voice within the case study—be as inclusive as possible. The more people quoted within the story, the more readers you will have.

Because our annual conference was looming, we set a submission deadline for case study entries. This encouraged customers to get the review and editing work done. Without a deadline, a case study can take months to pass the initial review, and within the contributor's company, delay edits and approvals. If a customer could not provide final approval for whatever reason (usually because someone within the legal or communication team determined participating was against a company policy), we leveraged all the work by creating an anonymous case study. The names of the customer and company would be deleted, but almost all the other information would remain the same, so the story was told but no one would recognize the company. As the old proverb goes: waste not, want not. We utilized anonymous stories as much as named stories.

We held firmly to the deadline so that Excellence Award committee member reviewers and judges would have time to submit their evaluations. Each committee member scored each story based on nine criteria developed by the committee. No case study was compared with another case study. Stories were judged on their own merit, each client's metrics of success, and their own level of information shared. To compare a large Fortune 500 company with a small 100-employee outfit would not be feasible or fair. Stories could be judged on strategy goals attained, clever tactics utilized, involvement of company executives, or even the degree of change management that the customer achieved. Judging criteria might even be different from one product category to the other due to demographic considerations.

Case studies were required to meet our standards for content length: no more than two pages and no less than one full page. For each case study, we required a challenge, a solution, and a result. Each entry had to be laid out in our case study template, have all the pieces of information we required within the story, and indirectly identify the capabilities of the product that we wanted to showcase. It was their story 100 percent, but it was influenced by us, written by us, judged by us, and promoted publicly by us.

When customers submitted an internally approved case study, it would be sent to our award committee for judging. Within five to ten business days, we surprised the winners with a special package that contained a Mylar helium-filled balloon on a ribbon that was tethered to the box so when the customer opened the box, the vibrant, congratulatory balloon floated out. The congratulatory package included a nice letter and a form that requested the names of client team members to be engraved on the awards. Clients also received promotional instructions about the award that would be delivered at the company biannual user conference. Separately, we sent a gift basket of treats to be shared among the winning team. We made a follow-up phone call and e-mail to the winners to confirm that they received the official notification of winning and encouraged them to return the engraving forms. I personally put together the winners' packages, printing all the materials off the office printer, getting the balloons taped down, and saving money by doing everything from our office instead of hiring a fulfillment shop to handle it.

At the award ceremony, we set up VIP tables for the award winners and spouses who were registered. Additional team members who attended cheered their winning colleagues. We scheduled onsite interviews with customers, which we videotaped. Our sales and marketing teams then used those videotapes as leverage with prospects and in campaigns. Many videos became the referrals needed during the sales process when a live customer referral was requested but not readily available.

Step Four: Create an Award Show to Highlight Winners and Spotlight Their Stories to Other Users for Cross-Selling Opportunities

In 2006, the company honored 18 businesses, agencies, and institutions for their outstanding use of information technology to reduce risks and costs associated with environmental health and safety (EH&S) and crisis management. The inaugural Excellence Awards celebrated extraordinary achievements of organizations that reduced operational risks, resulting in reduced costs and enhanced operating efficiencies. The 2006 Excellence Award winners were Alcoa, Inc., DAK Americas, Eastern Municipal Water District, Idaho State University, Linc Facility Services, Los Alamos National Laboratory, New Jersey Natural Gas Company, Northern Illinois University, Plant Services, Inc., Sunoco, Inc., SUPERVALU, Volvo Trucks North America, Inc., Halliburton, Hunter Douglas, United Stationers Supply Co., Puyallup Fire & Rescue, City of Boynton Beach, and New York Power Authority. One Excellence Award winner, the New York Power Authority, was recognized as the "Best of the Best"—this story stood out as the most innovative and generated the greatest benefit to its stakeholders.

Winners were determined by achieving measurable benchmarks for innovative use of technology, impact on employee health and safety, emission reduction, benefit to the surrounding community, cost reduction or fiscal impact, risk reduction, and internal awareness of the project.

I came up with the idea of the "Best of the Best" winner because we needed a grand finale and a degree of surprise to the event. Everyone coming knew they were winners. We needed a little extra surprise to encourage the audience, the winners, and the media to stay until the end of the show. The "Best of the Best" kept people interested.

Now that we had all our winners, we needed to publicly honor and recognize them for sharing their thought leadership. A tiny budget notwithstanding, we created a presentation show with lights, music, and dialogue. The script had details for all involved represented by color. As part of the finale, each customer walked across the stage to accept the award, was photographed with the CEO, and returned to his seat. The master of ceremonies was a staff member who got the room excited, got them laughing, and maintained the spirit of the evening.

We called to confirm each winner's attendance, and more than 50 percent attended. We had decided that, to save time, we would only tell the story of those winners in the room. We shipped awards to those who could not attend, along with a copy of the souvenir program and our regrets that they were not there in person. We e-mailed tracking codes so they could anticipate when their award would arrive.

The attending winners served as speakers for sessions during the user conference. The winners' sessions came ready-made with handouts of their case studies and were designated in the event program as award-winning sessions.

Every opportunity was made to share the award-winning stories. Each chair at each table had a booklet of all the case studies and a souvenir program that listed all of the winners. Partners and sponsors paid to be in the program booklet with their level of sponsorship. Customers scheduled time in the hands-on labs with sales and support teams to see the solutions that were highlighted in the case studies. Of course, we strategically seated award winners with prospects who were considering the solution for which the winner was being honored. A "winner's room" created a bit more of a VIP treatment with champagne and caviar to capture additional photos of the winners together with their awards. This also provided the media and partners an opportunity to meet the winners as well.

Step Five: Launch Post-Production Promotion

After the award event, the real work started. The company marketers moved quickly to update the company Web site during the night of the event to display the "Best of the Best" winner, as well as the other award-winning case studies. Winners were also identified on selected content Web sites such as *Pollution Engineering* and *Industrial Safety & Hygiene News* and other different media outlets.

We created a CSI-themed webinar that included many speakers who could share background information that detailed all the reasons why clients' projects worked well, and what role information management played in the success story. Winners became ready-made speakers with a case study handout and slides that highlighted their story. Overnight, we had 18 potential speakers to help us gain speaking sessions at events and conferences. After the award event, we started getting calls from the major technology companies such as Microsoft, IBM, and Oracle because our customers' case studies would briefly mention that our solution was aligned or integrated into theirs. This helped us earn "points" as a developer/business partner to these leading companies and increase our partnerships with them. We became "gold" or "platinum" partners with free access to better tools, thanks to the priority status we received because of our ability to share customer success stories that indirectly included them.

We pitched the stories to the media and offered interviews with our award winners and their executive team. We pitched the stories to analysts, giving them access to the winners and their executive teams. We created an award-winner Web page for all our winners to link to that explained the award program and served as their third-party validation of the work they were doing for their company.

Last, but not least, we sent handwritten thank-you notes to each winner, offering our gratitude for their participation.

Step Six: Create Revenue-Generating Alliances

From the beginning, I realized we would need a sponsor to give credence to our inaugural award program. I identified one editor from one media company with which we did lots of business. I created a business case to target him as our sole sponsor. He had two publications that matched our audience: *Pollution Engineering* magazine and *Industrial Safety & Hygiene News*. After discussing the idea of the program and the fact that it was connected to our annual user conference, he agreed to sponsor our award program. We created a barter agreement that benefited them and us. He was able to distribute his publications at no charge, was introduced during the event, helped judge entries, received direct access to winners in the private winner's room to interview, had his logos on everything at the award show, received an award to thank him for being our sponsor, had a reserved VIP table for him and any guests he wished to sit with, received a list of attendees, and was offered first opportunity to sponsor the event again next year. For our benefit, we got pre- and post-event full-page announcements about the award program and its winners, as well as Web banners to announce the award program. The publication and its staff provided third-party validation to the event. We saved time pitching our stories to publication because they were able to get the inside scoop by being judges; they preselected the stories they wanted to publish from all our different winners. The editors coordinated with us more and allowed us to work more as a team. They posted our case studies as content on their sites, linking back to us, which helped our SEO rankings. We created joint, free webinars with the editor whereby the publisher owned the list of attendees.

Many of the benefits just listed were not included in the business case I created to pitch the barter agreement. All these benefits and more have arisen as we worked with different sponsors. While at the user group event, the editor pulled me aside and said he wanted to be the sponsor for the next event. I told him that directly after the award show the previous night, I was approached by a software partner informing me that his company wanted to be the sole sponsor of next year's award show and would cover all its costs. Eventually, we worked out that there would be a media sponsor and a partner sponsor.

Along with the handwritten note that I sent the media sponsor, I provided a small post-event evaluation report regarding a few metrics of success. Results from our user group event survey had the award program listed as the highlight of the entire event, beating out our keynote speaker and daily sessions. Many comments from our attendees were "How can I get one of those awards?" Interest from other customers drove up participation to 43 award-winning case studies in 2008.

We knew we had a successful engagement program that we wanted to grow, but we didn't know the true value of it until we saw 100 percent of our award winners renew their service contracts with us—on time.

Highlights and Takeaways

The following are a few highlights and takeaways from this chapter:

- Thoughtfully recognizing your customers' successes brings huge benefits to almost every aspect of business.
- A well-designed and implemented award program makes it easy for your customers to create content that will feed collateral pieces that are tailored just for you.
- Engage your company stakeholders to get their insights and build allegiances and alliances to help sustain your program.
- Ensure that your program's accomplishments are measurable so you can demonstrate its value to your company.

About Barbara Thomas

Barbara Thomas (also known as BT) is the president of Creative Tactics, a Washington, DC, area marketing company that specializes in advocate marketing. She has an award-winning reputation (recent winner of the 2016 Killer Content award) for providing strategic ideation, effective creative marketing, and outstanding results. With over

25 years of marketing experience, she helps drive business growth, manage the marketing processes, and increase sales opportunities. She has worked in both the agency and corporate marketing arenas with experience in database management, list management, copywriting, graphic design, lead generation, social media, content management, and overall integrated marketing. Her industry strengths include automotive, aerospace, chemical, defense, energy, engineering, environmental, health and safety, financial, maritime, purchasing, software, supply chain, and technology. Barbara attended Madison Area Technical College, University of Wisconsin, and Virginia Central University. She is a former board member for Direct Marketing Association of Washington, DC. She is a Certified e-Marketing Professional (CeM) and Certified Direct Marketer (CDM).

Barbara Is an Advocate

As one of about 1,400 beekeepers in Maryland, she is an advocate for Burt's Bees products. From their lip balm to their lotions, she highly recommends the wonderful products. Because of these products and her parents' influence when she was younger, she became a beekeeper. For years, she has kept bees (both solitary and honey) in her backyard, helping to pollinate her neighbors' gardens and trees. Her home and hives are called "The Fah-Mas Hive." She volunteers to help educate the community and, with her husband, sells honey at the local agriculture county fair. The hobby of keeping bees was passed down to her by her father who kept bees—both honeybees when he was younger and solitary bees when he retired. She points out, if you prefer the taste of clover honey, try orange blossom, sage, or tupelo honey if you can find them locally—and always try to buy your honey locally. For those who like a heavier, deeper flavor, try buckwheat honey. Remember, life is always sweeter with a honeybee as a friend.

Endnotes

1. Understandably, the company and its account representatives resisted paying for case studies because revenue goals took the hit. In addition, paid advocates are really not advocates at all.

2. Bob Nelson and Stephen Schudlich, *1001 Ways to Reward Employees* (New York: Workman Publishing, 2005).

5

The Power of One Advocate

One person really can make a difference.

Today's successful marketing strategies are defined by their ability to drive increased business opportunities through promotional channels that generate thousands or millions of prospective customers. It is rare to find examples where a single person could make the difference between an organization's success and failure. Yet, that is exactly what happened when one dedicated consumer embarked on an ambitious campaign that enabled eBillingHub to dramatically transform itself from a company about to close its door into a leading provider of online solutions for electronic invoicing. The resulting relationship between supplier and its determined advocate demonstrated the power of public endorsements from a single satisfied customer, and how those endorsements can influence the success of a brand or product.

Greg Coticchia, cofounder of eBillingHub, said the start-up company began several years ago—with few customers and sparse revenues. As its meager performance persisted, managers searched for reasons why the company was unable to overcome persistent market barriers. Coticchia and his team wondered whether they had failed to execute their business strategy properly, or if the opportunity just was not there.

After a couple years and continued subpar financial performance, eBillingHub's leadership considered closing the business. However, in March 2007, they decided to launch one final effort to rescue the business from the dissolution by hosting an educational webinar:

eBilling: How to Gain Control of Your Growing Volume and Vendors. To ensure its success, eBillingHub's marketing team made two important strategic changes. First, they refocused the presentation to spotlight eBillingHub's capabilities for automating manual processes, a key differentiator that directly addressed customers' pain points. Next, they carefully targeted prospects specifically for the event.

Among the attendees was Peter Secor, an attorney from Choate Hall & Stewart LLP, a major Boston law firm. Although they did not anticipate the impact, inviting Secor would pay huge dividends for eBillingHub by launching a transformative one-person advocacy campaign that miraculously reversed eBillingHub's fortunes and started the company on a path to improved brand recognition and profitability.

Secor's law firm had previously used manual processes to support its billings. By automating those procedures, eBillingHub enabled the firm to reduce its operating costs and increase efficiency. When eBillingHub delivered on its promise of improved productivity almost immediately, Secor just as immediately became a powerful advocate to eBillingHub by sharing his company's success story as a customer reference and conference speaker. Secor also used his influence in online reviews and as a popular blogger.

Secor's relationship with eBillingHub was a near-perfect model of advocate engagement, particularly for an early-stage start-up trying to break through into a large marketplace. It was a perfect match: Secor needed eBillingHub's technology to drive process efficiency improvements and operational cost savings; eBillingHub needed a passionate advocate to tell its story in the marketplace. Secor's testimony carried great weight and influence in the industry.

Secor's advocacy was critical to eBillingHub's future success. His status as a thought leader made it safer for other companies to consider the company's solutions because he brought credibility when telling prospects about the product. In essence, Secor—the advocate—did eBillingHub's promotion with greater credibility and assurance than eBillingHub ever could by itself.

Coticchia even wrote in his blog that every company should build relationships with passionate supporters like Secor. That is particularly true when a company brings a new product to the marketplace, or introduces a different way of doing something. This helps to ensure that customers feel confident about trusting your products. A customer endorsement can also illustrate the value of your products. It's good to have someone available with a high level of credibility in your company's corner. Peter Secor provided the level of credibility that was key to eBillingHub's market success.

Ultimately, eBillingHub benefited from the old saying, "What others say about you carries far more weight than anything you say about yourself." Your company isn't promoting itself; your advocate is doing it for you, which builds buzz about your company in the marketplace. Secor proved this right.

Although Coticchia left the company when it was acquired by Thomson Reuters in 2011, he remains an eBillingHub advocate. Today, the company continues to meet the growing demand for technology that drives efficiency and cost savings. Its success highlights the importance of advocates and the difference they can make to a business.

An Emerging Approach to Marketing

Today, Coticchia shares his knowledge of advocate marketing principles at the University of Pittsburgh Katz School of Business by teaching business-to-business (B2B) marketing in the MBA program. Coticchia regards *advocate marketing* as an emerging term that encompasses concepts that are associated with integrated marketing communications. Companies can develop true customer advocacy programs because there are more tools at their control—beyond customer references and press releases—to influence customers, prospects, and stakeholders.

Although *advocate marketing* is not yet used widely in academic literature, the topic is discussed and case studies are dissected at length to review identification, assessment, management, and analysis of advocacy. Coticchia expects that advocate marketing will soon be formally embraced and categorized in academia. That will spark more discussion about the nature of advocate marketing, and those concepts will be leveraged and their influence tracked.

Even as students are preparing to advance advocate marketing strategies, Coticchia believes the practice has already evolved into a powerful force for business growth, thanks to the current generation of marketers who are leveraging the market's latest innovative technologies, including social media platforms, to create enhanced prospect engagement while removing barriers to sales. Advocate marketing is just one of many changes that are transforming modern-day marketing practices.

For instance, Coticchia described an eBillingHub prospect who, toward the end of a selling process, was collecting references. This client did not just want a referral from a customer who was using the product; he specifically asked for users in Kansas City. Although the product functions the same in any location, this client wanted that level of peer-to-peer validation in order to connect a referral who matched his organizational—and personal—identity. eBillingHub met that game-changing need.

New Technology Expands Opportunities

Coticchia believes that platforms such as LinkedIn, Facebook, Instagram, and YouTube are creating a democratization of the marketing process. Online marketing strategies and tools are driving down the cost of entry to get into a larger game, making it easier for smaller companies to compete against larger companies. Executing advocate marketing strategies becomes faster and more efficient, and there are more opportunities than ever to utilize information to increase business opportunities.

Customer advocacy doesn't usually happen on its own. Companies need to develop strategies that utilize tools such as social media to execute their objectives. Marketers also need to be aware that technology can empower buyers to become both advocates and detractors. Finally, technology is not the only answer: Companies need to pursue multiple channels of marketing—print, radio and television, and other media—to make sure their advocate's—and their—messages meet their targets.

Despite the dramatic technology changes of the past decade, integrated marketing tactics have not substantively changed, but the tools that implement them have moved far ahead, Coticchia says. In addition, social media and inbound marketing have given us new awareness tools. Even lead-generation tools enable us to better communicate and gain deeper awareness of the latest market trends.

Advocate marketing, in particular, provides new methods of going beyond traditional lead-generation techniques to incorporate inbound marketing capabilities that empower marketers to capture better leads. This can occur by cultivating more credible product reviews, securing more influential references, getting more productive customer feedback, and, importantly, sharing content with confidence.

Modern technology helps companies obtain many types of advocates: influencer advocates, industry advocates, or employee advocates. Whether the advocate's testimony is earned or it is provided as part of an agreement in which the advocate receives a payment also impacts that advocate's breadth of influence and persuasiveness.

An old maxim in sales is that everybody knows at least 250 people. The old rule of 250 goes back to how many people would show up at a wedding or show up at a funeral. Thanks to social media, people have a lot more acquaintances. LinkedIn, for example, records thousands of people who have more than 2,000 contacts. Klout, for example, takes the raw numbers and computes individuals' sphere and depth of influence.

However, Coticchia thinks the rule of 250 still applies because social media empowers the average person with the capability to influence that many people, and many more. Dedicated advocates for a product, brand, issue, or cause are probably influencing at least that many people within their personal network.

Highlights and Takeaways

The following are a few highlights and takeaways from this chapter:

- A single advocate helped eBillingHub transform from an underperforming start-up to an industry-leading technology provider.

- A new generation of independent-thinking, tech-savvy marketers is driving greater interest and awareness of advocate marketing across the business landscape.

- Advocate marketing is becoming recognized in academia as a unique form of marketing practice and research space.

About Greg Coticchia

Greg Coticchia is an award-winning technology executive with over 25 years' experience in high-tech products and services. He is considered by many to be one of the best strategic minds and marketing executives in the technology business. He has led or been a major contributor in two of the largest and most successful software companies in the world, Legent Corporation (now CA) and AXENT (now Symantec). Recently, as CEO and cofounder of eBillingHub, he grew the company from inception to establishing it in a leading market position that led to its sale to Thomson Reuters. Coticchia has played key strategic and leadership roles in 11 start-ups and founded 3. He has held executive positions for better than two-thirds of his career, participating in companies that range from $10M to over $1 billion in revenue. He has helped raise over $65 million in venture capital in his career, and has actively participated in over 17 mergers and acquisitions at both the company or product level. In the last 15 years, the companies that Coticchia has participated in have netted "exit valuations" of eight times the revenue on average, and 16 times the investment on average.

He has served as CEO (four times), president, and chief operating officer (COO) of several successful start-up companies, and has been involved or responsible for the launch of over 100 products, solutions, and companies. His publications and presentations on marketing strategy and product management have been recognized as both visionary and thought provoking by leaders in the technology business. Coticchia has served on many boards (including NFR, Four Rivers, and others), assisting senior management with strategic planning and other critical initiatives, and has been recognized for his work and contribution in his service to these organizations.

A graduate of the University of Pittsburgh in Industrial Engineering, where he also received his MBA, he currently teaches both business-to-business marketing and entrepreneurial leadership at the University of Pittsburgh Katz School of Business. He also attained certificates in Entrepreneurial Management from Carnegie Mellon University and in Professional Coaching from Duquesne University. In addition to his many recognitions and awards from the businesses he has served, Coticchia was named as a finalist three times for the Ernst and Young Entrepreneur of the Year Award and for the

Tech 50 CEO of the Year. Additionally, he was named a 2006 Distinguished Graduate of the University of Pittsburgh Katz School of Business.

Coticchia's particular specialties include the following:

- Experienced in leading and managing organizations during their growth in various stages, from start-up to $1 billion in annual revenue
- Proficient in leading, coaching, and teaching marketing, product management, sales, strategic planning, and business development in the commercial software and related high-technology business
- Skilled in introducing and positioning new products, companies, and strategies

Greg Is an Advocate

When asked, "What are you an advocate for?" he replied, "I'm loyal to many products and services, including the Nest Thermostat. In my experience, it is delightful, and an unusual pleasure for a routine household device because it's a really exciting technology that works well. It is elegant and simple and is easily installed. And the fact that you can take a thermostat and differentiate it from the rest of the market is just amazing."

He is just as passionate and discriminating about everything he believes in—his personal and professional reputation for integrity reflects it.

6

Breaking Past the "Press Release" Goal

Admit it. As marketers, we love it when a customer agrees to participate in a press release. We are thrilled when customers put their name close to ours—and they confirm in print that they like us! It doesn't seem to matter if the customer can only share a benign statement such as "We've done business with them." For some reason, we hang on to a need to share our relationship with the world through a press release—and here's the irony—that may never get picked up by anyone other than a search engine.

Marketers need an intervention that forces them to reevaluate the value of press releases and reassess how they are used through media properties and their audiences to spread a message. It is then a short leap to understand how advocate marketing provides treasured accolades that far exceed a singular press release. In modern public relations, it is not the story that matters so much as how the story is shared, posted, tweeted, pinned, and otherwise disseminated to reach as large and targeted an audience as possible. In fact, a study conducted by the Institute for Public Relations indicated that the influence of traditional mainstream news media continues to weaken.

According to the Institute of Public Relations, "...various new emerging and social communication media have brought dramatic changes to many aspects of public relations practice. Highlights of our 2014 results include Twitter narrowly replacing Facebook for the first time as the most frequently accessed new medium for public relations activities. LinkedIn and YouTube placed third and fourth. Google+ continues to struggle in these measures. For the third year in a row, our research found the influence of traditional mainstream news media continuing to weaken."[1]

Brian Gladstein, executive vice president of technology marketing at GYK Antler, shares one of his favorite stories about a client discussing how new customers contribute to his marketing efforts. The client boldly stated, "If we do not get a customer to participate in a press release, we believe we have failed at our job." He went on to ask, "How can we get more of our customers to participate in our press releases?" That narrow view seems to sum up how many traditional marketers define customer advocacy. However, Gladstein says that customers, given the right circumstances and incentives, can provide much more than simply putting their names and a quotation in a press release. There are many ways that customers can be involved as advocates to achieve marketing business goals. For more than four years, Gladstein has been helping businesses meet today's urgent market challenge: getting customers to become active and authentic promoters of businesses they rely on.

Specifically, he endorses developing advocate marketing strategies that build genuine customer loyalty and enthusiasm. That passion felt by the customer, when properly nurtured, can become a robust engine for support and advocacy that far exceeds the reach of most press releases. Brian's team at GYK Antler operates a broad range of programs that generate advocate engagement for their clients. Gladstein defines advocate marketing as

> ...an organized effort to get customers involved in the business beyond the traditional vendor/client relationship model in which a customer pays a vendor for a product or service.

Advocacy starts when a customer embraces the company's vision for that market. To Gladstein, good customer relationships are built for the long haul. The relationship must be authentic and mutually beneficial for both the company and the advocate. A sustainable relationship with advocates requires time and investment, but, in turn, advocates help sustain and build upon that relationship. For example,

Rapid7, a leading provider of information technology security solutions and GYK Antler client, coined the phrase "give now and receive later" to describe its unique approach to customer service. This has paid dividends for the company and its customers. The firm works closely with IT data security managers who typically shun opportunities to participate in public advocacy. Instead of focusing on news releases and case studies, Rapid7 developed a program that encourages industry peers to share best practices and help each other prevent security breaches. As a result, the company has attracted more than 400 advocates who promote their products and show other professionals how to optimize the use of its security software to prevent online attacks. Customers benefit from programs that highlight their achievements and opportunities to provide input into future product development.

Gladstein feels that it is important for customers to be invested in the company. To be sure, people may raise concerns about the appearance of asking a customer to do work for them. To those people, Gladstein suggests adopting a new point of view in which customers perceive their investment as part of a partnership with the business. When that occurs, they are more willing to go the extra mile to support the business. Both parties contribute and everyone benefits. The "give now and receive later" relationship usually results in a deeper level of loyalty that converts information into actionable engagement that drives advocacy.

According to Gladstein, customers fulfill their role as advocates when they provide the following:

- **Endorsements**—Customers vouch for you, saying great things both publicly and privately, such as sharing best practices in a case study or providing a public testimonial or a reference call. Participation in a press release also falls into this category.
- **Referrals**—Customers help identify new leads by referring friends, colleagues, and peers. In fact, 50 percent of

B2B marketers believe referrals were the most efficient lead-generation tactic, according to Chief Marketer's 2014 Lead Generation Survey. This indicates that motivated customers have the capability to unleash a powerful lead-generation (or a demand-generation) engine.

- **Education**—Customers teach your market by sharing experiences and expertise; this establishes thought leadership and frames the conversation. In this critical role, customers interact with communities where new buyers come to learn about products and solutions that are vital to their success.

- **Representation**—Customers provide intelligence, insight, and feedback on your market, and discuss their problems and how your products and services meet their needs. Customers are a valuable resource for generating new product ideas, as well as affirming an existing product feature. This helps to ensure that functionality and usability are aligned with market demand.

Today, Gladstein believes that it is critical that businesses connect with customers in ways that exceed the capabilities of a press release. Customers share their experiences on social media, and their feedback directly influences the way people make buying decisions. Successful marketing programs—especially for businesses that depend on recurring revenue—inspire advocates by engaging customers and providing an educational, rewarding, or fun user experience. In turn, advocates can help marketers connect with the organizations that traditional marketing practices would not otherwise reach. That's why advocate marketing strategies provide strategic advantages that exceed the value of the traditional customer/vendor business model.

Advocates Reach and Teach

An effective advocate helps fans reach and teach new prospects about your products and services. Advocates want to help others and share their knowledge of best practices to follow as well as identify mistakes to avoid. In addition, advocates can help marketers exceed account-focused relationships in order to reach customers in tight-knit professional communities. Sometimes people cannot give a public endorsement due to PR restrictions to legal constraints to simply a desire to remain out of the public spotlight. Innovative companies like Rapid7 have expanded their consumer advocate programs by creating social communities in which peers who manage sensitive information can learn from their shared experiences and exchange ideas. It is within those communities that advocates become heroes for brands on a broad scale.

Professional communities provide opportunities for advocates to share their experience with products and services in a closed or semi-private setting. Participants may share product information and their experience with it to help solve a peer's challenge, thereby taking a leadership role within the community. Advocates are very motivated to contribute to communities' ways that they cannot in their day-to-day setting. To reach those targeted personas, Gladstein suggests identifying communities where your targeted B2B professional is a member. That could be a more effective strategy to remove barriers to advocacy.

Advocacy Transcends an Open Support Ticket

Some marketers and salespeople seem to shy away from requesting a reference from customers who have open maintenance support requests. Gladstein is surprised when marketers or salespeople take that approach because it presumes that active support tickets will automatically generate negative customer reactions. He suggests that isn't always the case. He recounts the experience of an account manager who needed a reference from an IT customer. The account manager was ready to approach a customer who was perfectly suited to influence the prospective client, but hesitated when an open support ticket was discovered. However, he decided to approach the client anyway—and was glad he did because the customer was more than enthusiastic about providing a reference. Why would someone do that?

Gladstein cautions marketers not to automatically regard a support ticket as an indicator of a poor customer relationship. In fact, an open support ticket could mean that the customer trusts your company and support staff enough to solve system issues in a timely manner. That's an example of an advocate marketing program changing the paradigm around customer support because companies with active support tickets actually can be a better reference for your company if they believe that your business delivers fantastic customer support.

Creating a Top-Down Internal Advocate Culture

According to Gladstein, the most essential attribute to start and maintain a successful advocate marketing program is executive leadership. Top managers have the power to promote an advocate-oriented culture throughout the company. It is important that the CEO or executive sponsor reinforce the message that customers are critical for success. Gladstein understands that the CEO must plant the seed, but each business unit within the company must take the initiative to fully embrace and nurture that relationship through a customer-centric mantra. Momentum generally starts with account managers, customer support specialists, or customer success business units—those who are closest to customers on a day-to-day basis—and expands across to business line leaders who need referrals and case studies to support their sales within their domain. An example is the company's content team that manages webinars and special events where speakers can share their third-party experience for using the product to address a business challenge.

Customer relationships touch every part of your organization. Large companies that use traditional operating models have well-defined processes that dictate who is authorized to contact a customer, who owns the relationship, and how many times the customer is contacted by different parts of the organization. According to Gladstein, advocate marketing strategies challenge the traditional approach by taking a subset of customers and establishing new relationships that plug them into other customer-related business processes, thus taking a comprehensive approach to product development and go-to-market strategy.

Managing that kind of change isn't easy. Gladstein encourages companies to move slowly and adopt the strategic model used by Rapid7 by starting with an executive sponsor, a high-level, highly influential, visible leader who takes ownership for driving change. Executive sponsors not only inspire the organization to change behavior, adopt new practices, and modify its culture, but they also fight for the initiative among their peers at the executive level, all the way up to the CEO. They support the initiative from a political perspective, help to acquire resources and eliminate obstacles, and mentor the initiative's key change agents. A customer-centric leadership ensures that your company implements a culture that is open to change, and this from-the-top perspective is key to making it successful by sending a powerful message of support for an initiative or program of corporate-wide visibility and endorsement. Executive support also ensures other business units will lend support to the program.

Measure What You Manage

An emerging industry best practice for advocate marketing includes implementing technology to track and measure advocates' activities and preferences. Measuring customer feedback through defined and tested data points identifies how much progress is made toward customer satisfaction goals. Tracking of qualitative and quantitative metrics of success are vital to any program, especially the advocacy marketing program. Gladstein recommends that companies start by identifying metrics that align with measures of success used by their executives, even if this is difficult. Gladstein encourages companies to start with metrics that gain visibility and importance with top executives and are in line with the organization's operational goals, including the following:

- **Sales metrics**—The effect of advocate marketing strategies can be measured by identifying leads and sales that are influenced through campaign metrics or lead-generation metrics, such as influence on pipeline, on revenue, or on support renewals. By identifying deals that are impacted, companies can establish the percent of pipeline and revenue growth that can be attributed to your advocacy program.

- **Marketing metrics**—Gladstein recommends tracking marketing metrics, such as simple page views and downloads. If your advocates are publishing their own content, track how many leads their blogs are generating as a measure of their influence.

- **Internal metrics**—Customer success metrics, such as the Net Promoter Score (NPS) or internal metrics (e.g., membership rate or other customer satisfaction measurements), provide organization-specific metrics that gauge how you are meeting customer satisfaction and places to improve. Gladstein also suggests tracking the percentage of customers who are members of your advocacy program, as well as engagement rate and engagement frequency—how often they publicly advocate for you.

Those reliable metrics help track the success of the program itself. Choose goals and thresholds that the entire team can embrace and achieve in order to show that your company is engaging with customers in a meaningful way beyond simply participating in news releases.

Highlights and Takeaways

The following are a few highlights and takeaways from this chapter:

- Eliminate the belief that the end goal of advocacy is a customer quote in a press release.
- Advocate marketing strategies help build genuine customer loyalty and convert that enthusiasm into acts of support.
- Create an internal advocate culture from the top down.
- Adopt the "give now and receive later" attitude.
- Companies can validate the effectiveness of their advocate strategies by measuring a broad range of sales, marketing, or membership activities that are affected by customer endorsements.

About Brian Gladstein

Brian Gladstein is the executive vice president of technology marketing at GYK Antler, a full-service marketing agency that acquired his previous company, Explorics. Brian continues the work he started at Explorics, specializing in advocacy and loyalty marketing programs for the B2B high-tech industry. Gladstein has launched dozens of products, starting as a developer and evolving into a marketer after he realized he enjoyed talking to customers. He has held senior roles at RSA, Bit9, and several other Boston start-ups. Throughout his career, he has promoted the idea that customers are a huge source of untapped potential, and now helps clients grow by inspiring their customers to engage in acts of advocacy on their behalf. Brian is also a co-organizer of the Lean Startup Challenge, a six-week start-up competition in Boston based on the Lean Startup methodology by Eric Ries. Gladstein is an expert at applying Lean Startup, Customer Development, and Business Model Generation practices to both early-stage and growth-stage companies, and actively coaches numerous start-ups in Boston and beyond. Gladstein holds a bachelor of science in computer science from the Massachusetts Institute of Technology and a master of business administration from the Stanford University Graduate School of Business.

Brian Is an Advocate

"My wife and I are big fans of Trader Joe's, a popular grocery store chain. In particular, what we really like is the remarkable service that you get from the moment you walk in the door. It's like you're walking in and interacting with people who are like you. They like being there and really want to help. What makes us advocates, and not just happy customers, is how whenever we serve food from Trader Joe's, we always tell people where we got it from. We tell people to shop there. We genuinely enjoy being customers there and feel like part of their tribe."

Endnote

1. http://www.instituteforpr.org/examining-social-emerging-media-used-public-relations/

7

Overcoming Skepticism with Open Communications

What should a marketer do when the customer base and target audience include people who are better known for privacy and skepticism than for being enthusiastic brand advocates? That was the dilemma for Rapid7 (discussed earlier), a leading information technology security data and analytics provider of products and services that are widely used by IT security analysts and network administrators—just the people who do not like the spotlight. Engaging Rapid7's customer base of IT security professionals to leverage the benefits of advocate marketing was a strategic business goal the company's customer alignment and experience program manager, Evan Jacobs, wanted to achieve.

Jacobs met that challenge by implementing an innovative advocate marketing program whose success has amazed both him and his executives, thanks to strategies that have transformed customers into fiercely loyal supporters.

Open Communication, Not Bigger Walls

Rapid7's success can, in part, be attributed to its "Customer Success" approach. Whereas some companies take an insular approach to addressing growing IT security threats, Rapid7 has a more progressive perspective. They urge security professionals to share their knowledge and experiences with effective security tools and services with industry peers. "It's not just about building bigger walls around your company so it will be less likely to be breached than your competitors," Jacobs says. Rapid7 encourages customers to create a broader culture that maintains "We're all in this together so let's help each other fight threats while we're helping our vendor make better products." In the spirit of innovation and community-building, Rapid7 developed its online community—Rapid7 Community—that has empowered IT security professionals to share the latest industry best practices and help one another protect their digital infrastructures from ever-present threats. In addition, customer discussion forums have become a focal point where users publicly promote the benefits of Rapid7's products and share knowledge for optimizing use of the company's software solution.

Customer-Centric Approach Builds Customer Loyalty

"From its origins, being customer-centric has been imbued in Rapid7's corporate DNA," Jacobs said. The company believes that strong partnerships with loyal customers are as important to its market growth as its ability to deliver innovative products. In addition, he believes their customer-centric relationships go hand in hand with their approach to advocate marketing. Customers are rapidly becoming advocates for Rapid7 because of the value and benefits they receive that inspire loyalty and the desire to participate in news releases, video testimonials, or case studies. Through sharing information among themselves, customers attain a heightened level of understanding to leverage Rapid7's solutions to enhance their security posture and offer feedback for future enhancements to even better help them achieve their security goals. Through this engagement, customers help Rapid7 build better products and services because they benefit in the end.

One success that illustrates its customer-centric commitment is Rapid7 Voice, one of the leading vehicles through which customer engagement is delivered. With just over 10 percent customer participation, Rapid 7 Voice recognizes IT security professionals who both implement best practices—including adoption of Rapid7 technology solutions—and publicly share their success stories with industry peers. "Customers love the program," Jacobs says. Another aspect to the Rapid7 Voice program is that it provides customers with early access to new products and capabilities, and empowers customers to provide feedback on the company's products directly to engineers and product managers. The Rapid7 Voice program has grown quickly over the past few years, with more than 10 percent of the company's customers actively participating in the program.

Advocates Ensure Successful Product Launch

Rapid7 organizes customer teams under its Design Partner Program to provide feedback for a solution during its development journey. Rapid7 Voice's Design Partner Program lets customer partners provide early and direct feedback on new features being developed. This ensures that the voice of the customer is embedded in the product, which brings credibility and acceptance across industry peers. In effect, Advocate Marketing is Rapid7's primary road map for how it works with customer advocates. It provides value to customers by ensuring that their operational needs are met and deepens engagements. Only at this threshold does Rapid7 reach out to customers and ask them to advocate.

During a recent 18-month period, Rapid7 invited 12 customers to participate in the product development process from ideation to launch. Rapid7 was testing a new concept that was significantly different from its existing product line so the development team was interested in how customers, some of whom could become potential buyers, would react. Customer reaction was also valuable because developers could observe firsthand how frontline professionals interacted with the system, and whether the software features addressed real-life issues for participants. The solution eventually enjoyed a highly successful rollout, thanks in large part to customer input.

Following the rollout, some of the customer team members extended their advocacy efforts by speaking at Rapid7 road shows and customer conferences. This greatly increased users' confidence, knowing that the solution was tested by their peer frontline professionals who understand their operational challenges.

Jacobs says customer influence is important because IT security professionals are pressured to keep their servers and databases safe, and they depend on Rapid7 solutions to help meet that goal. Customers want to influence industry solutions because they want to make security products stronger, and by optimizing all of the solution capabilities to fortify their operations, industry solutions become more robust and comprehensive. Despite being under time pressure, a growing number of customers make the time to provide feedback because they love the product and want to make sure that it continues to meet their unique requirements.

Advocacy Options for Sensitive B2B Industries

Professionals who support B2B organizations that manage sensitive information (such as financial services, health-care providers, and law firms) are often barred from any mention in press releases or case studies. Many companies have strict policies that prohibit these professionals from speaking publicly about any aspect of their information security efforts, which includes mentioning specific vendors, tools, or technologies. However, Jacobs reminds marketers that there are many other alternatives to enable those professionals to become advocates, including the following:

- **Guest blogging**—Some companies have flexible policies around guest blogging or posting messages to social media platforms like Twitter and LinkedIn.

- **Closed-door speaking opportunities**—They can speak to groups that hold members-only meetings. In some cases, they can attend a meeting as a private citizen but cannot disclose their company title or their company affiliations.

- **Webcasts**—They can host a webcast, reaching a broad audience of current customers as well as prospective customers and others interested in emerging InfoSec topics.

There are many other creative ways that customers can operate within their corporate policies and still have the ability to speak publicly. They can be approved if the opportunity is presented as one in which speakers will share knowledge and best practices such as tips and tricks for optimizing their user experience with our software product. In fact, Jacobs says, some customers are grateful that Rapid7 helps them gain approval for an advocacy opportunity because they look forward to opportunities to share knowledge about the company's products as well as some background about their own security program.

Highlights and Takeaways

The following are a few highlights and takeaways from this chapter:

- Rapid7's advocate marketing program shows that a customer-centric approach to advocacy can inspire customer loyalty and encourage companies to participate in information sharing and product promotion.

- Customers who are invited to provide input into the development of new solutions help to ensure that the resulting product meets market demands. Those customers also promote the solution at road show events and user conferences.

- Professionals in B2B firms that handle sensitive information may be able to leverage other advocacy options, such as speaking at closed-door events or guest blogging if they are barred from public endorsements.

About Evan Jacobs

Evan Jacobs is the customer alignment and experience program manager at Rapid7, representing the voice of Rapid7's customers across the organization and building strong, meaningful partnerships that deliver value for the company's customers. In this role, Evan drives the customer engagement strategy with an emphasis on creating deep understanding between the company and its customers to benefit all parties. This includes ideation, design partnership, and beta programs, as well as user groups and customer advocacy programs. These engagement programs now involve more than 10 percent of Rapid7's customer base, and were integral in bringing two brand-new security analytics solutions to market in late 2013. Prior to joining Rapid7, Evan was in strategy consulting for five years, most recently as a senior consultant with Peppers & Rogers Group, a boutique consulting firm solely focused on customer-centricity. Evan holds BA and MBA degrees from Columbia University.

Evan Is an Advocate

"For a long time I had heard about Wegman's, but until recently there weren't stores in my local area. I had heard that they were legendary for having great service and for just being a fun place to shop. They finally opened a location in the Boston area that is close to where I live. When they opened, there were a couple thousand people lined up outside the door, even in rainy weather. I finally had the opportunity to see it for myself. Now, I will talk them up to anyone. It's more fun shopping there than at any other chain. That elevated shopping experience made it more fun. Now it's a box you've got to check on your weekend to-do list. It has shaken up the market in this region. Wegman's has redefined what a great place to shop is. They have elevated the standard."

8

Innovative Marketing Strategy Propels Intel to Successful Global Product Launch

In 2012, Intel, one of the world's leading providers of innovative computing technology, was preparing to launch a new line of tablet computers. Tablet industry sales were soaring, experts were predicting a strong growth trajectory, and Intel officials saw tablets as a natural extension of their business. Even though it possessed valuable assets, including a highly regarded global brand, Intel would be launching new products into a highly competitive market in which industry leaders Microsoft and Samsung were among the businesses already well established in the consumer tablet market.

Sandra Lopez, director of marketing for new business at that time, was tasked with leading the effort to promote the company's new tablet product line. An award-winning marketer known for her entrepreneurial spirit, Lopez had an impressive track record for launching new initiatives during her ten-year tenure at Intel. Scott Jaworski, Intel's head of buzz marketing for the company's new business organization, was selected to manage the program.

As they developed strategies for the product launch, Lopez and Jaworski recognized that an advocate-focused strategy, with social media engagement and outreach as its foundation, would play a central role in the plan to introduce Intel's tablets. They discussed possible strategic approaches: Should they create content to distribute through existing social platforms or recruit advocates to create their own content to share their stories? After deep risk-to-reward strategizing and cost-benefit analysis, they selected the latter alternative.

Intel has already invested considerable energy to expand and leverage social strategies internally and within its market. The company had already incorporated two-way communication into its corporate marketing toolkit as part of a commitment to be a leader in social media. In addition, Intel marketers discovered that a cohort of online brand advocates was already posting valuable feedback on online forums.

Lopez' vision was to create a campaign that was creatively disruptive, and not dependent on cost-prohibitive media. Instead, Intel chose to unleash an army of advocates to share product information. The goal would be to show the value of Intel tablets to thousands of prospective buyers online via Twitter, Facebook, YouTube, blogs, and other social media sites—a kind of virtual flash mob.

The campaign was based on a simple underlying principle: Empower advocates to share their story and let Intel's product stand on its own merit. Lopez believed Intel's advocates could provide a competitive advantage by becoming a de facto sales and marketing channel for the company.

To support the program, Lopez and Jaworski enlisted two sets of advocates: nearly 75 external bloggers, each a well-known domain expert, and nearly 350 volunteers from Intel's workforce. Leveraging influencers from verticals other than marketing sent a powerful message that Intel tablets could deliver value to audiences across a broad spectrum of interests.

Jaworski also organized teams of employees, armed with appropriate training, to create buzz around Intel tablets by engaging consumers on leading social platforms. The program allowed Intel colleagues to step away from their day-to-day routine and transform themselves into an army of enthusiastic online brand advocates. Eventually, the almost 350-employee team became known as the "Tablet Smart Squad" in recognition of the immense talent of Intel's staff. Team members completed a three-part training curriculum to ensure they understood overall strategy, value proposition, and product features. Intel's training ensured compliance with rules adopted by the Federal Trade Commission (FTC) for employee-driven advocacy programs. The FTC requires companies to train brand advocates on product features and capabilities to avoid making false or misleading claims. Advocates are also required to disclose their relationship with Intel, in accordance with the requirement that employees reveal any material relationship, including employment, that they have with the product or brand they promote.

The program, which began as a pilot, enabled Lopez and Jaworski to show that advocacy campaigns could be an effective way to launch new products. In addition, Lopez and Jaworski decided to test the Tablet Smart Squad's ability to help drive sell-through to retail outlets by amplifying retailers' promotions that were supporting Intel-based tablets. After providing guidance on the promotion itself, they simply asked the Squad to help promote it. Within 24 hours, they advised the Squad to stop the promotion because the campaign had quickly achieved its objectives—to drive sales.[1] Overall, it was clear that Tablet Smart Squad advocacy can work.

In addition, the team created a Twitter hashtag, #TabletTipTuesday, that encouraged and enabled anyone to share a tablet application tip on Tuesdays. This provided a natural platform for participation by Intel's partners and its internal advocates. In addition, they created the hashtag #IntelTablets to track social conversations.

During its two-year existence, the Tablet Smart Squad campaign brought increased visibility to Intel tablets across seven countries and nine social networks, and clearly demonstrated that a company's employees can serve as an effective marketing channel. The campaign's success generated several more requests from Intel businesses to launch other new products. To date, Jaworski has guided about 12 Tablet Smart Squad teams that have helped Intel businesses create buzz for a variety of new product lines.

In her new capacity, Lopez is responsible for new Intel product launch promotions for the Wearable Tech in Intel's Fashion business line. To be sure, she continues to adapt and support the Smart Squad philosophy by emphasizing the importance of influencers, advocates, and loyalists in the fashion vertical.

Due to its great success, Intel has received a number of prestigious awards from respected marketing organizations, including the American Advertising Award,[2] formerly called the Addy, and the 2013 Hub Prize, gold level,[3] which validated the success of Intel's advocate marketing strategy. In particular, *Hub Magazine* applauded the campaign for "Excellent use of the most important resource of any company—its own employees." In addition, Lopez received the 2013 Marketers That Matter award.[4] Not surprisingly, a member of a judging committee, a senior-level marketing executive for a leading furniture company, approached Intel team members about adopting the Smart Squad concept.

Other measures of the tablet campaign's success included external influencers and Smart Squad teams that delivered a combined audience of 4 million people, while producing nearly 85,000 online activities, which generated an estimated 49 million impressions.

Smart Squad's Success Goes Beyond Marketing Achievements

Beyond its marketing achievements, Smart Squad also proved to be a major employee relations success as well. Intel has more than 100,000 employees across facilities in 46 countries. The company's massive scale makes it nearly impossible for an individual employee's contribution to be visible at the consumer level. In fact, there's a risk that some people can become siloed and personnel teams fractured. Smart Squad brought together participants from 20 different Intel business lines. Accustomed to working anonymously to support development and production of Intel technology, employees found themselves engaging directly with customers, and providing product information and other insights that promoted the advantages of Intel technology. Some had to overcome a lack of experience on engaging social media—one employee remarked that his granddaughter helped him create a Twitter account so he could participate. Jaworski was amazed at the level of passion and interest demonstrated by Intel employees brought together from a range of disciplines and pushed to the front lines where products are activated and deployed.

Today, the Smart Squad footprint extends from North America to markets in Europe, the Middle East, Africa, and mainland China; this poses some unique cultural and political issues for Intel marketers. Jaworski said Chinese audiences are less apt to speak candidly about a private organization. Instead, they use aliases. Social channels are more suspect. Still, they were able to influence audiences in that region.

Several Intel veterans told Jaworski that participating on Smart Squad was the first time they felt like they were contributing to the company's bottom line. Marketing Programs Manager Sylvia Salazar was one such example.

Salazar joined the Tablet Smart Squad while serving as a product marketing engineer. It was her first opportunity to interact directly with consumers and educate them about Intel technology. Like many of her colleagues, she was excited for firsthand exposure to prospective buyers. She created YouTube videos about the different Intel tablets on the market and provided content that articulated critical differences between Intel tablets and its competitors'. Those videos started several online conversations—and offline too. According to Salazar, some people who saw her posts on Facebook or Twitter would approach her at the gym. One person told her, "Hey, my mom is thinking about a Windows tablet and I saw your video. Now she's getting an Intel-based Windows tablet." Being recognized as an Intel staffer never happened before when she worked on other product teams.

Salazar's Smart Squad experience has influenced how she now approaches her work. In her current role as a marketing programs manager, she produces internal marketing programs to educate employees about a variety of Intel products and how they perform. Salazar said her Smart Squad experience alerted her to the need for internal marketing programs for employees that now support new program volunteers.

One of her greatest challenges was to create video content that was compelling enough that people would watch it, short enough to be effective, but long enough to be informative. One of the videos that Salazar produced featured time-lapse photography of three tablets, each running full-feature films. The video starts with fully charged tablets, and then shows how many full-length feature films can be played on each tablet. To meet real market needs, Lopez believes the video content rings true to everyone who travels. As someone who often takes coast-to-coast flights, she knows this firsthand. One of the most popular questions consumers will ask is "How many movies can I watch on this device? How long can I watch TV?" Creating that video was a clear-cut way to answer the question.

Divisions Between Traditionalists and Advocate Marketing Proponents

Lopez said the Smart Squad's emergence as a key marketing tool has helped generate considerable interest from other Intel business lines that want to implement advocate marketing strategies. Increased demand has also divided promotional professionals into two distinct camps. The first are social media advocates who believe that two-way communication is driven by online brand advocates; this camp represents the new wave of marketing. The second is the traditional marketers who believe direct mail, space ads, and other forms of marketing lead the campaign and Smart Squads complement the traditional forms. Traditionalists are not sold on advocate strategies because they believe promotional performance should be measured by widely accepted metrics such as gross rating points (GRP). In addition, they prefer to give spokespeople scripts rather than play-books. When marketers place an advertisement on television, GRP tells them how many people were reached. Lopez said marketers who embrace advocate marketing strategies, powered by activity on social media platforms, believe in the mantra "do more, go fast, get creative, embrace the power of social media and what it can do for your company's bottom line." More and more of these cutting-edge practitioners believe socially driven advocacy can generate a "positive network" effect—the power of one user to impact the perceived value of that product to other people. Studied and verified through inde-pendent research, over time, the positive network effects help create a bandwagon that more and more people join. Lopez acknowledges that social media metrics in marketing are in their infancy; there is not yet an accepted measurement that equates to GRP. That leads tradi-tionalists to question the value of social media's impact. One thing is certain, however—keeping an open mind and willingness to try new marketing tactics and techniques is crucial for success in any business.

Overall, Lopez says, Smart Squads have become great case stud-ies for other organizations that take Intel's advocate marketing play-book and build their own programs. The first step is for marketers to trust their colleagues and provide adequate employee training to ensure they can be successful and compliant with legal requirements. Marketers are accustomed to using platforms such as Facebook, Twit-ter, LinkedIn, and Pinterest. However, many nonmarketers may not use social media channels regularly, so it was essential for Lopez and Jaworski to provide a support structure where employees could obtain answers at all hours regarding Intel tablets as well as how to use social media applications. Infrastructure for the advocates was key for their success and the campaign's success.

Smart Lessons Learned

After two years of successful Smart Squad implementations, Lopez and Jaworski came away with several key takeaways. One takeaway is that money makes a person lazy. From a marketing standpoint, Lopez contends a big budget does not guarantee success. Success requires that marketing professionals must be super creative and be aware of every possible asset in terms of communication channels. Overcoming the lack of resources requires creative tactics. Also, understanding the consumers—especially advocates—is critical at a fundamental level. They have the capability to help achieve breakthroughs to increase product recognition and strengthen the corporate brand.

Jaworski added that when addressing new marketing challenges, he now always begins by asking, "How can I bring in influencers to tell the story?"

Highlights and Takeaways

The following are a few highlights and takeaways from this chapter:

- Lacking resources for a traditional advertising campaign, Intel marketers developed an award-winning, creative advocacy marketing strategy to introduce a new tablet to the market.

- Smart Squads that included advocates helped Intel promote new tablets on social media platforms, generating 24-hour sell-out situations with retailers.

- Thousands of impressions from potential buyers across diverse interests generated excitement among longtime employees and made them feel valued and special.

- Keep an open mind to new tactics and techniques because you never know where the next strategic marketing idea will come from.

About Sandra Lopez

Sandra Lopez joined Intel in 2005 as a B2B integrated marketing manager. Leveraging her rich and proven marketing experience within the technology sector, she quickly began to transform B2B marketing. She was then chartered to drive Intel's Consumer Marketing Strategy group, from which she led Intel's focus on the Masterbrand, Intel, as well as the launch of the award-winning campaign "Sponsors of Tomorrow." Recently, Lopez focused on launching Intel's first smartphone and Android-based tablets. Currently, she is responsible for driving Intel's Wearable Business Development Strategy within the fashion vertical. She has been a leading voice on driving the convergence between fashion and technology.

She has been recipient of several accolades: 2013 Marketers That Matter, Cannes Lions, David Ogilvy, Effie, Addy Awards, and Intel's Achievement Award.

Prior to her tenure at Intel, Lopez worked at Macromedia as senior director for Macromedia. Before that, Lopez served as marketing manager with Computer Associates. She brings over 17 years of experience in marketing within the technology and fashion sector.

Her tenacity to deliver impact extends beyond the walls of Intel. Lopez is a member of the Hispanic Association on Corporate Responsibility: Corporate Executive Forum—a program that provides the most senior Hispanic corporate executives at Fortune 500 a forum to discuss business issues, challenges, and solutions, and provide mentorship for the next generation.

Sandra Is an Advocate

Sandra is an advocate of WUNWUN—What You Want When You Want. Its concierge delivery services have made life more convenient for her and her family. There are situations in which Lopez needed to get product from point A to point B within an hour in the same city; WUNWUN made it happen. Or, when she is too busy to pick up groceries, she can request WUNWUN and have the goods delivered within an hour—giving her the time to focus on her family.

About Scott Jaworski

With more than a decade in interactive marketing from major Web sites to grassroots social campaigns, Scott Jaworski is a strategic leader who knows how to get things done. Jaworski joined Intel in 2011 as a marketing manager for AppUp. As director of AppUp.com and its social footprint, he focused on customer acquisition. In just one year, Jaworski was invited to join the Intel Ambassador program and was tapped to head buzz marketing for new business. In this role, Jaworski led internal and external social influencer programs aimed at having a lasting impact on Intel's consumers. Today, Jaworski can be found on a team leading Intel's global digital and social strategies.

Before he joined Intel, Jaworski served as director of interactive marketing and technology for HookUp Feed, where he led its technology team and served as chief strategist for all Tier-1 accounts; his clients included the likes of Aramark, Sam's Club, and Pier 1. Preceding HookUp Feed, he served as vice president, interactive services for Posner Advertising and managing director of interactive marketing and creative services at Global Fluency. He has also held senior positions at MortgageIT (a Deutsche Bank subsidiary) and CNN.

Scott Is an Advocate

"The product I am a devoted advocate for is Burton. Burton, a snowboard and apparel manufacturer that originated in Manchester, Vermont, was started by Jake Burton, a fellow Northeast snowboarder and one of the sports pioneers. As a young kid, I would go to the 'local' Burton shop in Manchester where I would buy demo boards that the Burton team riders (whom I aspired to be) were testing. The first time

I put a (Burton) board to my feet was in 1990 at a local Vermont mountain—Stratton. I've been riding Burton exclusively (Cruise 165, M8, PJ, Air 6.1, Twin 158, BMC, and Custom X) and have since started purchasing their garments and gear. Having been snowboarding in Europe (Switzerland, Italy, and Austria), British Columbia (Whistler and Blackcomb), and across the majority of our own U.S. mountain ranges, I think it's fair to say I've done my fair share of stress testing Burton products, and they haven't failed me yet. Thanks to their high-quality products, great customer support, and business values, consider me a lifer. Thanks, Jake!"

About Sylvia Salazar

Sylvia Salazar joined Intel in 2003 as a software engineer in the Technology and Manufacturing Group and currently works as a marketing programs manager for the Client Computing Group. Salazar is known for her creativity and out-of-the-box thinking, especially when it comes to looking at fresh, compelling ways of delivering messages and demonstrations, and clearly illustrating product benefits to her audience. She loves to learn new things and loves to share her knowledge with others. She uses these talents to lead creative marketing efforts around some of our coolest PC products and technologies. Salazar is a graduate of the University of Miami.

Sylvia Is an Advocate

"I'm a huge advocate for a workout company called The Bar Method. It's a bar-inspired—not drinking bar but a ballet barre—workout. It's a combination of yoga, Pilates, and dance conditioning. I started doing it over three years ago and it completely transformed my body. I lost eleven inches in less than three months. I've seen how it transforms not only people physically but also mentally. You learn that you can push yourself beyond the limits you initially set for yourself. The community is also very strong; I've created some amazing friendships with some of the other women. It's also very interesting to me that it's a very low-impact workout. I'm an indoor person, so I don't like going outside even though I live in Oregon. I like working out in an air-conditioned room indoors. You don't sweat very much and it's turned me into a morning person. So I usually work out at six o'clock in the morning, which means I have to wake up at five. It's very Zen for my mind; it quiets my thoughts so I can get a workout in, and then I can calm my head and shut it down a little bit for an hour. And then I come out and I'm calmer; I can see things a little bit differently. I'm constantly talking about it on Facebook. I actually used to be an instructor, but I had to stop because it interfered with my Intel work. I have to travel too much for Intel work and I couldn't keep teaching."

Endnotes

1. Lopez cautions the sell-through could have been impacted by many other variables, including the retail sales price (RSP) or the terms of the promotional offer itself.

2. American Advertising Awards are sponsored by the American Advertising Federation and recognize the creative spirit of excellence in the art of advertising.

3. Hub Prize is sponsored by *Hub Magazine* in recognition of excellence in the brand experience. Submissions are judged based on whether the brand experience served a purpose, solved a problem, and made everyday life better for people. http://www.hubmagazine.com/hub-prize/

4. Marketers That Matter is sponsored by Sage Group and *The Wall Street Journal* in recognition of Bay Area marketing leaders who lead and inspire teams, innovatively engage customers, and leverage new technologies to drive success. http://www.marketersthatmatter.com/award

9

Citrix Moves from Customer Content Factory Model to Content Showroom

CIOs make purchasing decisions 25 percent faster when they're supplied with a reference, according to a 2010 Gartner report.[1] Customer references are one of the best marketing tools a company has at its disposal, but many organizations aren't tapping into the power of this resource. There are a couple of reasons why. Either they don't know how to start or they don't have resources to do so. How many times have you read an article in which the company tells you how terrific its products and services are but nowhere can you find verifications from its customers? Companies can say anything they want, right?

"Nothing sells better than customers selling to other customers." This is one of Lee Rubin's favorite phrases from his senior vice president of sales at Citrix. Rubin, senior manager of the Citrix's Global Reference Programs, is a member of a highly successful team that has implemented a wide range of advocate marketing strategies that are helping Citrix successfully market its products across the globe. In fact, Citrix was named *Program of the Year for Customer Experience & Account-Based Marketing* at the SiriusDecisions Summit 2015. By providing innovative technology solutions, enabling more than 330,000 organizations worldwide to work more effectively, Citrix is a top industry performer with 100 million users globally and 2014 earnings of $3.14 billion.

"Our customers talk about the products they use every day," Rubin said. "They provide firsthand, trusted, and vocal feedback about our company and our products. And they're more valuable to us than any advertisement that we could buy."

Citrix's Community and Customer Marketing Infrastructure

According to Rubin, the secret to the company's success is equally simple: His team delivers customer stories to account representatives at the moment in the sales cycle when they're needed most, moving from a customer content factory model to that of a content showroom. By delivering customer stories to the sales representatives throughout the selling process, they win more deals and close them quicker. This has a positive bottom-line impact for the program and the company.

Citrix's Community and Customer Marketing infrastructure has four primary areas:

- **Community programs**—Coordinate user groups, online communities, and the Citrix Technology Professional program

- **Reference programs**—Include the sales and marketing help desk, reference database management, and Customer Reference Forums

- **Strategic customer program**—Takes responsibility for advisory boards, recognition programs, advocacy, and producing all customer videos

- **Content marketing**—Develops case studies, customer slides, infographics, and e-studies

The Citrix Community and Customer Marketing team work with nine industry verticals and five overarching product groups, each overseeing three to five products. Rubin's team tracks the Reference

Engagement Value (REV) of the programs throughout Citrix's sales pipeline. The REV measures the value a reference has within the pipeline to influence and help close a deal to a successful win. In 2014, Citrix's REV equaled $500 million from the marketing efforts of Rubin's Community and Customer Marketing team. This was a 40 percent increase compared with the prior year. Additional 2014 year-end metrics confirmed that over 2013, a 150 percent increase in sales reference utilization, a 133 percent increase in marketing reference utilization, and a 67 percent increase in closed/won revenue.

Rather than just creating a video or a written case study, Citrix leverages the content and repurposes it to use for other areas, creating a full bill of materials (BOM), including a video, the case study text, a list of approved quotes, and a hundred-word executive summary of the case study that the public relations (PR) and analyst relations (AR) teams use to help pitch stories for customer interviews. They also craft social media text (which generates hundreds of social media impressions), infographics, e-studies, presentation slides that can easily slip into a sales representative's presentation deck, and product spotlight text.

Rubin's content team members work with about 12 customers each quarter on a case study. Typically, a case study may take as long as three months or more to complete due to the need to finalize customer reviews and approvals. However, Citrix creates a 100-word executive summary within 48 hours of an interview. This executive summary allows the communications team the ability to start pitching the stories immediately so that stories are not embargoed while waiting for PR or AR to pitch them. This saves time, eliminates delays, and keeps everyone enthusiastic throughout the engagement experience—especially the customer. Delays can sometimes equal derailments and/or disinterests.

During the program's early stages, Rubin says the team focused on producing content. Citrix now calls it The Content Factory, and it delivers content—684 reference assets—conveniently via an online search capability searchable by product and industry. Rubin and his eight-member team are responsible for references and testimonials. His team provides a reference help desk where they help stakeholders address more complex requests.

Implementing and Leveraging Customer Reference Forums

A key element of Rubin's reference strategy is the quarterly Customer Reference Forum, which is an invitation-only, online roundtable discussion moderated by Citrix's thought leaders. These are aimed at deals in the pipeline that are at 60 percent of the sales cycle or higher, and are designed to help the sales teams close deals and win contracts. The Customer Reference Forum session begins with a moderated discussion featuring a Citrix customer followed by a Q&A session with the attendees. Customers do not give a presentation; they simply talk about how they evaluated, implemented, and/or use the Citrix solution. Registering attendees are asked to send questions in advance so the customer can address their queries as part of the discussion. Held as a webinar, this is a low-cost effort whether one person or a thousand people attend. The session is recorded but not shared openly online for the public. The recording is sent to those who registered to attend but, due to one reason or another, could not attend. Ideally, they will hear the questions they hoped to ask in the recording.

Since Citrix started holding quarterly Customer Reference Forums, requests for live one-on-one customer reference calls have dramatically decreased. Previously, at the end of every quarter, Rubin's team fielded nearly 50 requests each month for peer-to-peer calls. On a given quarter now, they get about 4 requests.

Creating the Content Showroom

Rubin's team received recent feedback from salespeople that current processes and tools were hindering their ability to access content. The sales representatives use tablets and smartphones while out in the field visiting prospects and need to be able to access customer evidence anywhere and at any time. So Citrix recently launched a new reference database tool.

In partnership with Salesforce.com and Ethos, Citrix is developing a new reference application that is tile-based and allows its sales reps to see all the references located in the database. When they click into a reference record, they get rich, detailed information that combines reference record and account information.

Rubin says, "Citrix is moving from the content factory to a content showroom with this new program." By moving away from its Share-Point sites to an application that is embedded into Salesforce.com, this one-stop reference tool meets sales representatives' needs. The content showroom contains everything pertinent to their sales team, including information on Citrix solutions, products and services, competitive intelligence, customer references, win wires, win-loss reviews, industry analyst reviews, field management, and partner information.

But Rubin's team didn't stop there. They worked with Citrix enablement to create Citrix Sales IQ, which Rubin declares is the genesis behind showcasing content at the right time. Citrix divided the sales cycle into different segments. At each segment, the team recommended appropriate resources that can be used based on what might be happening at that point. Sales representatives answer a series of questions based on the current sales stage. Those answers create the opportunity to deliver relevant reference content right when the sales representatives need it. For example, for deals at 10 percent, a suggestion is made to sales to use Citrix's Work Better videos—polished, high-level, commercial-quality videos that tell how customers are using Citrix products to improve their business operations. At 25 percent, a suggestion is made to representatives to use the e-studies and infographics. At 40 percent, Citrix Sales IQ suggests that the representative use the Top 150 slides. At 60 to 75 percent, suggestions are made to invite their prospects to a Customer Reference Forum.

Citrix has thousands of happy customers, thanks in part to its Customer Reference program. With more than 600 enthusiastic reference customers, they have lots of opportunities to share their views on Citrix products with prospective customers. Citrix customers are enthusiastic advocates; they look forward to opportunities to share.

Highlights and Takeaways

The following are a few highlights and takeaways from this chapter:

- If you can validate return on investment (ROI) with a customer's endorsement, CIOs report they make purchasing decisions 25 percent faster when supplied with a reference.

- Deliver customer stories to account representatives at the moment in the sales cycle when they're needed most, moving your customer marketing program from a customer content factory model to that of a content showroom.

- Track your Reference Engagement Value (REV) of your program to measure the value a reference has within the pipeline to influence and help close a deal to a successful win.

- Implement a Customer Reference Forum to reduce peer-to-peer reference call requests at the end of each month or quarter.

About Lee Rubin

Lee Rubin has more than 20 years of experience in corporate marketing and nonprofit leadership. He is an avid social media devotee with more than 2,100 friends on Facebook, 2,700 connections on LinkedIn, and a Klout score of 60. A demonstrated leader in marketing and brand strategy for leading technology companies, including France Telecom, Digex, Savvis, and Citrix, Rubin has served on the national board of governors of the Human Rights Campaign and was board co-chair of the National Gay and Lesbian Task Force: Foundation. He currently serves on the board of directors for Our-Fund, a Fort Lauderdale-based community foundation.

Lee Is an Advocate

Lee Rubin is an advocate for LGBTQ (lesbian, gay, bisexual, transgender, queer) equality. He chairs the LGBT employee resource group at Citrix, in Fort Lauderdale, Florida, where he is senior manager, Global Reference Programs. In February 2015, Rubin's efforts were recognized by South Florida Gay News in its "Out 50," a list of the top LGBTQ leaders in the community. He is currently on the Board of Directors of Our-Fund, a LGBTQ community foundation, and has helped to raise more than $150,000 for Pride Center of South Florida. In 2009, he was elected co-chair of the National Gay and Lesbian Task Force Foundation, and in 2010, was appointed chair of the National Gay and Lesbian Task Force's 401c3 Action Fund. Rubin previously served on the National Board of Governors of the Human Rights Campaign (HRC). He also writes a monthly blog (http://lgbtsfaevents.blogspot.com) highlighting the events of LGBTQ nonprofits in Fort Lauderdale, Florida.

Endnote

1. Gartner 2010—www.gartner.com

10

The Influential Power of Customer References

No one knows your customers like you do, and building this knowledge is likely the most influential investment you have made in your business. The critical tool—the technology "Swiss Army Knife"—for advocate marketing is the customer relationship management (CRM) system. A CRM helps you record, store, track, mine, and analyze the invaluable and irreplaceable information about your customers' needs, histories, and concerns to help positively grow your relationship with them. Using CRM solutions intelligently can help align customer information with your business goals for superior predictive planning and modeling, in short, to meet everyone's needs. There are a number of CRM systems on the markets; one of those is the Customer Reference Program, which is, specifically, a customer reference platform.

Customer references are an important component of advocate marketing and a vital tool that sales teams use in many ways to meet many goals. Potential buyers frequently seek advice before purchasing products and services; trusted references can increase sales as well as build current and potential customer trust in your business itself. A well-coordinated customer reference program can realize big profit-promoting benefits, such as the following:

- Spending less time searching for suitable references
- Avoiding overuse or underuse of valuable references

- Gaining and assuring authority and credibility with prospects
- Reducing sales cycle times

Neil Hartley, founder of Incubatus, LLC, believes that customer references are the primary mainstay that impacts buyers' decisions. Salespeople regularly rely on customer references for peer-to-peer validation that ensure that deals get done.

Customer Advocate Versus Customer Reference

Hartley says the terms *customer advocate* and *customer reference* are sometimes used interchangeably but actually represent distinct customer personas. He defines an advocate as a stakeholder who proactively champions (and defends) brands, products, or services in public and private forums without a request from the company itself. In contrast, a customer reference is a brand advocate who responds to requests for a wide variety of endorsements, including peer-to-peer calls, news release quotes, testimony for case studies, or video interviews. Of course, a person can be both an advocate and a reference.

Get Organized and Proactive

Hartley advises that companies adopt practices that organize customer reference processes into a proactive program that is supported by technology and is a part of the company's strategic business plan. He believes that too many companies take a reactive approach by relegating customer references to the end of the sales cycle; this leaves companies vulnerable to last-minute requests that sometimes catch salespeople unprepared. Proactive use of, for example, customer stories and quotations earlier in the sales cycle helps build trust and mitigate a buyer's risk.

He believes a buyer's journey may not be linear and may not follow a well-understood process. Hartley rightly asks, "Why apply rules to what prospects or customers can or can't do?"

Many companies assume that buyers know what they are doing, but actually, they may not have experience procuring technology and certainly do not know, or care about, your sales processes. They undoubtedly are not aligned with your well-ordered, well-documented linear sales path. Buyers understand their business and, usually, their needs but should not have to be students of your preset sales funnel processes. If a buyer prefers to talk with a live reference earlier in your structured sales cycle, they might be conducting a lot of research on their own and getting to a buying decision earlier than the sales representative expects. But the typical reaction from sales is to say, "No, you can't do that until we've gotten past step five of our seven-step process." Hartley thinks leveraging marketing automation or even automating sales pipeline rules that are built in to customer reference management systems are common mistakes based precisely because buyers do not know your processes—nor should they have to. Hartley advises that if a prospective customer passes the evaluation phase and enters into the making decision phase without your sales representative's help, then embrace the speed of the closed purchase order.

This scenario is all too common: After the parties have agreed on price and project specifications (and the salesperson believes that the final agreements are at hand), the customer suddenly requests to speak directly with a client reference. Too often, Hartley says, the response resembles a fire drill, starting with an urgent e-mail blast to the sales and marketing teams that requests help to identify clients whose persona and customer experience closely align with those of the prospect. Businesses that manage customer references with ad hoc processes expose themselves to multiple risks, especially reaching out to the same clients for references repeatedly, causing reference burnout. Ad hoc arrangements, according to Hartley, too often result in "happy" reference customers eventually becoming "annoyed" reference customers.

A growing number of companies have embraced technology platforms that streamline and organize processes for recruiting and providing customer references. These solutions help salespeople quickly identify clients who are available and authorized to speak as a reference and, more importantly, have not been "overused." These solutions help companies avoid reactive, panicky exercises and, instead, respond efficiently and confidently by identifying all appropriate customer reference resources available with a few keystrokes. A customer reference platform also provides approval workflow and tracking that mitigates risks, prevents reference burnout, and enables a company to efficiently manage marketing support materials, such as case studies, customer quotations, white papers, video testimonials, and other corroborating, persuasive materials. Tracking usage of these materials thus enables ROI calculations that were previously difficult to establish and glean insight on which materials contribute most to sales success.

The Golden Circle Philosophy

Why do some leaders or companies inspire while others cannot? Hartley believes that while trying to engage clients to become advocates, companies should consider an approach developed by Simon Sinek, author of *Start with Why*. Hartley cites a study by Sinek that concludes that successful brands such as Apple and great leaders such as Martin Luther King focus on the *why, how,* and *what* of their business rather than the *what, how,* and *why*. The successful leaders and companies think from the inside out rather than from the outside in. And this creates the "Golden Circle."

People prefer to do business with companies that share similar core beliefs. Sinek claims "People don't buy what you do; they buy why you do it." Sales representatives who explain the cause, purpose, or core beliefs of the company and why it exists are far more compelling and successful than sales representatives who explain what the product does, how it does it, and why it does it. The latter sells the steak; the former sells the sizzle. Although many customers claim that their buying choices are based on the benefits that products' or services' features and capabilities bring (i.e., the product's *what, how,* and *why*), Hartley believes that customers who become strong advocates make buying choices based on why the company exists (its mission or vision), how it plans to achieve its goals, and what products it offers that help make those goals possible—the *why, how,* and *what.*

Hartley believes that Sinek's Golden Circle affords a significant opportunity for those producing customer stories of many types because these advocates speak to the *why* rather than the *what.* By aligning a company's core beliefs along the model of this Golden Circle, magic will happen.

Does Social Selling Make the Best Advocates?

The process by which a customer introduces someone in her network—typically a client or industry peer—who may be interested in a company's products or services to that company is called *social selling.* This is another way that customers serve as advocates, according to Hartley. Inspired by concepts from *Influence: The Psychology of Persuasion,* written by best-selling author, psychologist, and marketing expert Robert Cialdini, social selling is based on the premise that people are more likely to be persuaded to consider a product or service if a person of trust introduces them to a respected authority figure in that space. For example, if someone introduced a business partner or friend to a colleague who is an authority on marketing, that person is more likely to be receptive to the expert's message than if that expert introduced herself without the introduction. The recommendation of an expert by a trusted colleague helps overcome doubts that occur during cold calls or other forms of initial, anonymous contact. Because of the trust of the colleague that is conveyed, resistance is dramatically reduced during social selling introductions. When advocates are properly engaged, their social network becomes a powerful lead-generation engine for you and your company.

Highlights and Takeaways

The following are a few highlights and takeaways from this chapter:

- Customer references are a mainstay of an advocate marketing strategy. This peer-to-peer tactic can significantly influence customer decisions.

- Companies should consider the prevailing best practices for customer references, such as adopting strategies that organize information assets for prompt retrieval and ensuring that clients are not overused or overburdened in endorsing a product, service, or brand.

- Being proactive in using customer references can build trust and mitigate a buyer's risk.

- Social selling can be an engine to drive lead-generation growth by engaging customers to introduce "experts" to industry peers and clients that may be interested in a product or service.

- A strong advocacy mechanism includes leveraging a customer reference's social network to build trust and credibility to a wider but trusted pool of prospects.

About Neil Hartley

Neil Hartley has served in technology sales and marketing positions for more than 20 years. He has held several leadership positions, ranging from CEO of a high-tech start-up (Leximancer) to the United Kingdom manager of SPSS (which has been acquired by IBM). Neil earned his sales spurs during a 5-year tenure at Cadence Design Systems. Having developed a passion for all things customer satisfaction and customer advocacy, Hartley cofounded Riding High Rocks in 2015.

Neil Is an Advocate

"I'm a superadvocate of ASICS, Southwest Airlines, and National Car Rental. Southwest because I grew to love the no-seat policy, which initially seemed bizarre because I didn't know what was going on. I love Southwest because it's very cost-effective, booking is easy, and changes are free. The same applies to National Car Rental. You just turn up and choose a car. It is so simple. There is no checking-in. After a couple of months' worth of trips, I suddenly earned enough points for its executive-level customer reward program and now I could choose from the really nice cars. Which one do I want this week? Do I want a sporty car? Do I want a big car? A white car? A black car? A red car? I could choose whatever vehicle I wanted.

"Finally, if an overpronator were to ask me what kind of running shoe to buy, I would absolutely say they need to buy an ASICS shoe. I tried all kinds of shoes and only ASICS shoes are, as far as I'm concerned, truly designed for runners who overpronate. That's why I'm an advocate for those three companies: ASICS, Southwest Airlines, and National Car Rental."

11

Award Engagement Program Helps Win Two-Million-Dollar Contract

In 2008, Reid Hawkins was one of the top account executives with Environmental Support Solutions (ESS), a boutique environmental health and safety (EHS) software company. He faced a major challenge trying to win a contract to implement an enterprise-wide EHS software platform at PepsiCo, one of the world's largest food and beverage conglomerates. Hawkins had successfully navigated his proposal through the early procurement stages. As the competition and deadlines escalated, he faced a pitched battle with SAP, the world's leading provider of business software, to win the contract.

Regardless of their size and valuation, businesses are cautious about making major capital investments. When a company considers making high-dollar, high-impact, and sometimes high-risk expenditures for infrastructure and products, the timeline of the sales cycle lengthens, even when those changes are imperative to business sustainment and expansion. EHS software systems perform thousands of complex calculations based on inputs from hundreds of in-house and remote automated and manual systems. Thus, installation and effective use requires seamless integration across the disparate systems that support a company's multiple business lines. To ensure compliance with stringent government regulations, voluntary industry standards, and corporate commitments to reduce safety-related workplace incidents and lower environmental emissions, the accuracy of the EHS system calculations must be fully trustworthy and defensible.

Hawkins needed to inspire PepsiCo's confidence that ESS products and services could both meet PepsiCo's requirements and deliver long-term value. In every way, ESS' proposed solution was well suited to deliver on PepsiCo's business requirements. But to win the deal, Hawkins needed to devise a strategy to overcome SAP's global reputation and overwhelming marketing resources. He decided an in-person customer referral meeting would provide the best opportunity to underscore ESS' competitive strengths. But this would not be any ordinary in-person customer referral meeting.

Under normal business conditions, arranging such a meeting is nearly impossible. However, Hawkins had a significant advocate customer event he could leverage to his advantage: the ESS Excellence Awards.

Awards Transform Clients' Attitudes

ESS' chief marketing officer and associate vice president of marketing created the Excellence Awards in 2006 to recognize organizations for their innovative use, knowledge, and experience with EHS technology to implement industry best practices, improve productivity and operations, or meet compliance and sustainability goals.

In the past, ESS sales and marketing struggled to persuade clients to share their success stories for public distribution. To fill the endorsement gap, ESS published a handful of case studies each year. But getting case studies to publication was a difficult, protracted effort. Customers had difficulty getting approvals from internal corporate communications, or were simply not motivated to share their stories. In short, ESS users just didn't see what was in it for them. But when learning about the ESS Excellence Awards program, many clients' attitudes changed. Customers suddenly embraced the opportunity to share their achievements for an ESS Award nomination. Between 2006 and 2009, more than 80 clients submitted high-powered case studies to win the ESS Excellence Award.

Customer Referral Meeting Provides Powerful Endorsements

Before the conference, Hawkins learned that three of ESS' top clients—Alcoa, Duke Energy, and Spectra Energy—had been selected as award winners, and each would be attending the annual ESS user conference and award ceremony. Each company planned to send a group of frontline EHS managers to accept the award. Alcoa's delegation also included the vice president of their global EHS team, further enhancing the group's stature. So Hawkins reached out to his customers at Alcoa, inviting them to attend a private dinner that coincided with the ESS conference. He also invited the members of PepsiCo's purchasing evaluation committee, as well as his other award-winning customer, Spectra Energy. Each company's representatives agreed to attend the private dinner meeting.

The award presentation and dinner meeting had a powerful effect on the PepsiCo committee. They had an opportunity to hear the success of several award winners who had leveraged ESS software to address operational challenges similar to those that PepsiCo sought to address through its technical solicitation. Most compellingly, the PepsiCo team could personally ask questions of the Alcoa and Spectra Energy teams at the private dinner meeting. Instead of learning about the software's capabilities from a proposal or product brochure, the PepsiCo evaluation team met face-to-face with peers who relied on the software to support their operations and had made them successful in reaching their business goals. There is no better endorsement than real-world experience.

Once the meeting began, Hawkins provided some brief introductions for those in the room, and then left so his clients and prospects could talk privately. At first, he was nervous because the fate of the deal was out of his hands. Unsupervised customers could have delivered negative comments that could have prevented ESS from securing a PepsiCo contract. However, Hawkins remained confident of securing the deal because the software solution delivers good value through a reliable product, the PepsiCo team had witnessed an award gala that highlighted the success of many companies that use solution as a critical component of their operations, and Alcoa was known to be a strong advocate for ESS. When clients are successful and have received good value from a product, they willingly share their news of their success and purpose. In fact, Hawkins had previously invited customer advocates to provide references, presentations, and other activities with good effect during all stages of the sales cycle. He was ready to leverage his advocates again on such an important deal in hopes his strategy would pay big dividends.

And it did. The strategy worked perfectly. PepsiCo executives got the answers they sought, and Alcoa and Spectra Energy provided candid assessments about the capabilities of the software solution. As a result, Hawkins was eventually rewarded a deal worth $2.1 million with PepsiCo, one of the largest in the firm's history. Years later, Hawkins looked back and called the achievement a minor miracle.

Program Boosts Customer Advocates

ESS Excellence Awards attracts top corporate decision makers to attend the gala award ceremony, which is held in conjunction with annual ESS' users' conference. Executives and managers take great pride in being recognized for business achievements that might have otherwise gone unnoticed within their own organization. To be recognized and praised by industry peers is very gratifying and inspiring to the award nominees. One customer was so elated about receiving an award that she brought her mother to the ceremony that honored her work. In addition, the program increased attendance to the users' conference because award-winning organizations bring their colleagues and prioritize the conference in their annual budgets.

For executives, the award is an acknowledgment that the organization's investment in information management delivered on the promise to drive improved business performance while meeting the operational and financial goals. Whereas most corporate leaders are focused on revenues, margins, profitability, and share price, the award program recognized people who support those strategic goals and make sure that the organization maintains a license to operate, keeps insurance rates low, reduces their environmental impact, and maintains compliance with regulations and standards.

Award Program Elevates Sales Performance

The ESS Excellence Award program had a significant impact on Hawkins' career, too. The PepsiCo deal helped him achieve sales of $4.7 million in 2008. He was recognized as the leading ESS account representative, was awarded shares of company stock, and was promoted to vice president of sales. In addition, 280 of 500 audience attendees at the 2008 ESS Excellence Award ceremony were Hawkins' clients. The award program's biggest benefit, in Hawkins' opinion, was its ability to help close sales deals. It also helped him cement long-term relationships with clients. "It's not just about closing the deal," he contends. It's about being viewed as a trusted advisor or strategic partner, and having those relationships deep within their company. Any top-notch account executive who approaches his chosen profession seriously relishes developing the deep, strategic relationships that transform customers into advocates.

When asked what aspect of the award program surprised him the most, Hawkins pointed to the impact winning an award had on the companies that were recognized. He identified the renewal of their annual software maintenance contract. He informally analyzed maintenance contract renewals over three years and the results were surprisingly consistent. Award-winning customers had a 100 percent renewal rate during years in which an award program was held, and the rate dipped below 100 percent during the year that a ceremony was not held.

An award program helps increase customer loyalty ratings by double digits.[1] According to Hawkins, the award program provided access to powerful corporate authorities who had previously avoided his meeting requests. Before the award program, the only way he met with high-level executives was when there was a technical problem in the software solution. But, after meeting at the award program, that executive who had ignored Hawkins' meeting invitations in the past participated in several reference calls over the subsequent two years. As a result, that customer helped drive more software sales than any member of the firm's sales team.

The award program also paid dividends after the award ceremony. Hawkins said PepsiCo had a long-standing reputation for declining speaking opportunities at trade shows. The year after PepsiCo won its ESS Excellence award for its success, the company agreed to speak at a major industry conference to present the global benefits of its implementation project. That's why Hawkins regarded the ESS Excellence Award program as the gift that continually delivered sales and marketing benefits.

Advocacy Strategy Helps Drives Sales Connections

Hawkins has developed his own advocacy strategy based on a mix of customer references and marketing content to build a connection that is nurtured throughout the sales cycle. His approach consists of the following:

- **Case studies**—At the beginning of the relationship, he presents case studies that address the prospective client's business challenge.

- **Benchmarks against peers**—He follows the first case study with success stories in which the customer's performance can be benchmarked against industry competitors.

- **Recorded customer endorsements**—Next, Hawkins presents more personalized content, such as audio or video client testimonials.

- **Customer referral**—He arranges customer reference meetings when the deal is ready to close to completion.

Companies Should Incentivize Promotions

Hawkins believes it is a missed opportunity when vendors don't incentivize their sales and marketing teams to pursue advocate marketing strategies. It can be extremely difficult to get any organization—both buyers and sellers—to consent to sharing a significant accomplishment in a news release, social media, or a case study because some customers are opposed to publicly promoting their vendors. For example, Hawkins brokered a software sale and obtained approval for a news release from the company's purchasing officer and the operational manager. However, that arrangement was subsequently vetoed by the corporate communications officer and legal counsel. As a result, vendors often feel they have to make financial concessions to customers—which can cost thousands of dollars—for a news release announcing a sales win. This antiquated structure discourages sales professionals from pursuing promotional activities because their pay is reduced when clients agree to a discounted deal.

Highlights and Takeaways

The following are a few highlights and takeaways from this chapter:

- An advocacy strategy enabled an IT company to overcome a larger competitor to win a record-setting contract.
- An innovative award program generated dozens of case studies and helped drive up attendance at an IT company user conference.

About Reid Hawkins

Reid Hawkins specializes in leading and developing high-performing sales teams and managing accounts at Fortune 500 and Global 500 companies. During a career spanning more than three decades, he has helped several information technology companies meet or exceed their revenue goals. He is known for building collaborative client relationships and for delivering million-dollar transactions for software services and content, while competing against the world's leading technology companies. He also delivers a wealth of market and application experience in business intelligence/analytics, web conferencing, environmental/health/safety, compliance, MDAP (mobile development application platforms), and EAM/plant maintenance.

Reid Is an Advocate

"I'm certainly an advocate for some of the charities such as The Nature Conservancy and the National Resource Defense Council. I'm a big advocate for those organizations in their fight to preserve the ecosystem and the environment. I'm also an advocate for Ford. I've been a Ford guy for many years."

Endnote

1. Based on measurements found in *The Loyalty Effect: The Hidden Force Behind Growth, Profits, and Lasting Value* by Frederick F. Reichheld and Thomas Teal (Boston: Harvard Business Review Press, 2001).

12

Enthusiastic Advocates Help Businesses Drive Measurable Marketing and Revenue Performance

Jim Williams is an advocate evangelist who is passionate about telling marketers about forward-thinking organizations that harness the power of advocate marketing programs to advance their marketing and revenue goals.

Williams, vice president of marketing for Toronto-based Influitive, believes that most businesses today only identify a few customers who are fans of their brand, products, or services. But leading-edge companies are adopting scalable advocate marketing strategies supported by emerging technology solutions. They are identifying crowds of brand advocates and leveraging the passion of their fans into action that generates measurable benefits.

Every organization has known advocates, Williams maintains. He believes that for every advocate you know about, there are probably three or four yet to be identified. If asked, many would gladly participate in your marketing programs.

First, you have to learn how to identify your advocates. Second, you need to learn what motivates them to publicly endorse your brand. Finally, you want to align their efforts—and your own—for maximum impact on your marketing and sales objectives.

To ensure that your advocate marketing program will enjoy long-term success, start by asking yourself and your colleagues the following questions:

- Why do your customers advocate for you now?
- How can advocates generate more leads and Web traffic for you?
- How does it enhance your brand perception?
- How can they shorten your sales cycle?
- How can you keep advocates engaged with your brand beyond the first big push?
- What's in it for your advocates?
- How can you get your entire organization aligned around advocacy?

Advocates Pay Big Dividends for Savvy Firms

According to Williams, SMART Technologies is just one example of a firm that gained big benefits by implementing a strategy that developed and nurtured relationships with its brand advocates. SMART selects an elite group of advocates to participate in an ongoing customer engagement program to learn more about SMART's solutions, network with other advocates, and market the company's offerings to new prospects.

SMART Technologies, based in Calgary, Alberta, provides high-tech interactive whiteboards and projectors for businesses and schools that gained immediate traction. However, early market success was followed by unique challenges. The company found that it lacked resources to provide consultants and a professional services team to meet burgeoning demands for aftermarket services.

Given a seemingly impossible task, Deena Zenyk, SMART's senior advocate marketing manager, quickly devised a creative solution. She developed an elaborate strategy to identify and recruit teachers and other school officials to become SMART's training and marketing consulting team.

Zenyk publicly encouraged educators to perform a wide variety of education-based tasks, but what she really wanted them to do was host small, group gatherings of teachers and educators to learn best practices for using the company's products so they could get more value in the classroom. More than 400 school officials around the world responded to Zenyk's appeals. They later reported that they were motivated because they loved the technology and felt that they had a stake in ensuring the company's success. Teachers invested several hours learning about the technology and its application in schools. Then, as volunteers, they returned to their school districts to train their peers on best practices for the classroom, and by doing so, indirectly promoted SMART products to prospective customers.

She also used creative incentives, such as awarding points toward higher status within the customer community, and access to SMART's product development team to provide product feedback, to keep advocates active and engaged.

The program paid big dividends for SMART. Zenyk estimated that each advocate delivered services that would have cost more than $130,000 if those functions had been provided by full-time consultants. She also gained added value by presenting performance information to SMART's top executives and governing board to justify funding the program. And the program proved that SMART's products meet real, market-driven needs.

SMART supported its advocate program with an Influitive software solution called AdvocateHub that enabled Zenyk to track and monitor advocate data so she could efficiently nurture multiple relationships across its customer base. Prior to implementing Influitive's software application, SMART communicated with advocates through manual processes and e-mail—an approach that lacked a systematic method of aggregating and interpreting educators' data. Now Zenyk knows the right advocates to contact when she needs support for client projects. In return, SMART rewards willing volunteers with an experience that's enjoyable and gives them immediate feedback. Williams said advocates receive some form of acknowledgment every time they volunteer to perform a task. Williams says each acknowledgment keeps advocates engaged because they feel appreciated.

Another advocate marketing success story spotlights DocuSign, one of the fastest-growing cloud software companies and a provider of electronic signature technology and digital transaction management services. In December 2012, DocuSign launched AdvocatesHQ, an advocate marketing program for customers and partners that enhanced social media engagement, while boosting online consumer reviews and generating customer referrals. DocuSign was looking to generate more product reviews from customers on Web sites such as AppExchange, Salesforce, G2 Crowd, and Software Advice in order to increase its market visibility and sales opportunities. According to Meagen Eisenberg, DocuSign's vice president of customer marketing, the company earned a return on its investment in less than six months. Today, DocuSign attracts an estimated 40,000 unique users to join the DocuSign Global Network every day, and its advocate marketing program has been transformed into a revenue engine that has moved more than $3 million into its sales pipeline.

Influitive doesn't just promote its advocate marketing software to its prospects; advocacy is at the core of everything the company does from marketing to sales to customer success to product development. Because customers are a central marketing focus for Williams' marketing team, it spotlights the successes of marketers like Zenyk and Eisenberg, and positions them as the company's most valued assets. An innovative advocacy program shows appreciation for customers by publicly promoting their customers' accomplishments in ways that may positively influence their careers. For example, Influitive posted a "LinkedIn recommendation" that trumpeted SMART's advocate marketing success to Zenyk's LinkedIn profile. Also, Influitive's advocates are offered opportunities to speak at professional conferences where they can share testimonies about the advantages and challenges of their advocacy programs.

Surprising Benefits from Advocacy Programs

Advocate marketing programs often provide a variety of pleasant surprises in addition to meeting their initial sales and marketing goals, according to Williams. Raving fans never fail to amaze marketers by exceeding expectations to demonstrate their support of their favorite brands. Here are two examples:

- **Product surveys**—Advocates are more likely to thoughtfully respond to surveys and feedback requests than to special promotions that offer free items in exchange for submitting contact data. Williams believes this is because advocates want to feel like they are a part of the company and so happily provide information without remuneration.

- **Branding feedback**—When companies consider a new product name, changing a product's direction, or launching a major promotional campaign, they can count on advocates to strongly voice their opinion before those changes go to market. Williams believes including advocates in the decision-making process helps transitioning and accepting the change go a bit smoother.

Many organizations face challenges similar to those met by SMART and DocuSign that can be effectively addressed with an advocate marketing program. For example, when a company announces a product launch, advocates can generate hundreds of new referrals in a very short time. Because advocates are already committed to supporting the brand, they are always ready to enthusiastically endorse new products and services from a company they love—but only if the new product is good. Advocates will not support a bad product because they have their own reputations to protect. In addition, a request for referrals is often welcomed because of the strong vendor/customer relationship that has developed over time. Because the request comes from a trusted source, advocates are ready to share their enthusiasm with others. Sales records do not provide any clues that indicate which clients would be willing to provide a peer endorsement for products. This lack of customer-focused data can lead to account representatives repeatedly calling on the same customers for endorsements, causing referral fatigue. An advocate program can solve this problem: Businesses that invest in advocate marketing constantly collect, maintain, and monitor customer data. This guarantees that a list of ideal reference candidates is always available.

Some businesses struggle to create effective customer referral programs because they lack critical insights that would increase participation. Williams believes most programs are either poorly timed or awkwardly constructed, or they primarily rely on a form letter to generate customer interest; these approaches rarely connect with target audiences. Poorly designed programs do not clearly illustrate the benefits of making a referral or what will happen once a referral is provided. There are just too many unanswered questions to spur action, so appeals for referrals are unanswered.

The best-in-class technologies provide immediate acknowledgment to advocates when a referral is provided. They alert advocates whenever their referrals are contacted, and when a deal closes. This not-so-subtle reminder underscores that referrals are important to the advocates.

Williams loves when Influitive's customers launch an advocate marketing program using AdvocateHub and expect social sharing or product reviews, but get a big surprise when they receive referrals as well. Peers and friends are being referred and, in turn, they willingly contact the company for more information on products and services.

A Growing Interest in Developing Advocate Marketing Programs

As more buyers move to online transactions, advocate marketing strategies can significantly influence purchasing decisions across the global marketplace, Williams says. A growing number of potential customers now expect product or service ratings from existing customers, and will factor rankings and reviews into their overall buying decision. Momentum for customer advocacy programs is being driven by several emerging trends, including the following:

- **Rating platforms**—The increasing popularity of customer rating platforms, which enable them to share their opinions and experience with a product, give buyers the opportunity to circumvent traditional sales and marketing efforts until a later time.

- **Disruptive marketing**—Williams says customers are willing to change vendors at the drop of a hat—if the offer is right. If the cost and risk to switch is low, and the customer does not feel any loyalty, the renewal will not happen. As a result, businesses need to be aware that customer engagement is a key market differentiator.

- **Customer obsession is on the rise**—CMOs are constantly looking at strategies, including advocate marketing programs, to improve customer engagement. Companies operate at a considerable disadvantage when they fail to cultivate enthusiastic brand advocates. The best way for a business to closely align with client needs is for it to build an organizational structure focused on product offerings, along with consumer education and technical support. Once those investments are in place, companies can easily identify fans best qualified to speak publicly about their product experience.

Williams believes that not only do technology companies fail to manage customer relationships in a manner that inspires jubilant support, but they also do not optimize the impact of their happy customers.

Highlights and Takeaways

The following are a few highlights and takeaways from this chapter:

- Advocate marketing is an emerging necessity for every marketing department, which empowers companies to harness the energy and enthusiasm of their happiest customers to expand their marketing capabilities and drive increased referrals and revenue.

- Successful advocate relationships require significant engagement, so that customers feel appreciated and involved in the business.

- Customer-focused data provides critical insights that can help sales, marketing, and product teams inspire advocates to take action.

- Marketers are often surprised to find that enthusiastic advocates are willing to go to great lengths to continue the success of their favorite products and brand.

About Jim Williams

Jim Williams is a veteran marketer who is focused on high-tech start-ups. He loves bringing transformative concepts to marketers. Before joining the Influitive team as vice president of marketing, he held marketing leadership roles at Eloqua, Unveil Solutions, Lernout

& Hauspie, and several public relations agencies. He directs most of his energies toward ensuring that his two kids have a fantastic and memorable childhood.

Jim Is an Advocate

"I use a tool called Snagit all the time. This widget, produced by TechSmith.com, enables me to easily capture and manipulate screen images. I use it for basic image editing because I have no idea how to use Photoshop. When I need an image for an e-mail or a PowerPoint presentation, I use Snagit. I use it nearly every day. I love that it's easy to use, yet powerful enough to do the things that I want it to do. I've told many people about Snagit.

"Yet I think it's funny that Snagit has never reached out to me and said, 'Do you love our product? Would you be willing to recommend Snagit or write a review about it?' If they did, I would say 'Yes. It's a part of my day-to-day habits.'"

13

The Paradox of "Do as I Say, Not as I Do"

How do companies that encourage customers to provide testimonials, case studies, and referrals explain why they bar employees from providing testimonials, case studies, and referrals to vendors? The simplest answer is that most companies are structured autocracies or have an autocratic leadership that makes policies. And with autocracies, the golden rule is always "Do as I say, not as I do."

Every company wants advocates. Companies reap value when advocates publicly praise them about their products and services. They develop strategies and programs to encourage customers to publicly endorse or advocate for the company. But when it comes to their own employees, public endorsements, or providing positive praise for vendor products and services, internal legal counsel or communication directors prevent them. Why does this paradox exist?

"Because" Is Not an Answer

So why do companies continue the irony of the "Do as I say, not as I do" policy?

For some industries, it's the law. Advocacy is regulated. The Securities Exchange Commission (SEC) Regulation of Advertising by Investment Advisers is one example. The SEC Advertising Rule (17 CFR 275.206(4)-1) specifically prohibits an investment adviser from publishing, circulating, or distributing any advertisement that:

- Refers to any testimonial concerning the investment adviser or any advice, analysis, report, or other service rendered by such investment adviser

- Refers to past specific recommendations of the investment adviser that were or would have been profitable unless the investment adviser complies with certain conditions

For some companies, it is easier to say "no" to employees than to take on the risk, liability, or cost of letting employees provide testimonials, case studies, or referrals according to some directors of communications and internal legal counsels. The time involved in prepping employees for interviews or reviewing materials from interviews interrupts the billable work of internal legal and marketing teams. Their planned days would unexpectedly shift when needing to review the content to make sure:

- Whatever is written or said aligns with corporate messaging; all key departments need to be in alignment (for example, in a financial firm, Market Analyst Relations needs to be in sync with Investor Relations).

- No corporate proprietary information is shared and/or any competitive or industry information is inadvertently made public.

- Risk is minimized and liability is obviated.

- No statement is made as an endorsement on behalf of the company. Personal opinions must be explicitly identified as those of the individuals and not the opinions of the company. Some companies may have policies that prevent even personal endorsements.

With the expansion of social media, it has become more and more difficult to restrict employees from becoming advocates. Social media muddies how restrictive company policies can prevail over individuals' personal expression. Due to the multiple marketing channels today, companies find it more and more difficult to restrict employees from serving as advocates for a brand or cause.

It's Just Business

Lawrence Dietz, general counsel for TalGlobal Corporation, provides his legal counsel and market research analyst perspective.

TalGlobal offers security services ranging from executive protection and workplace violence mitigation to data forensics investigations. One service provided is analyzing the security design for buildings and complexes for risk analysis. During the course of these assignments, Dietz confidently says the company's managing directors would have been asked to endorse products or services used. In practice, TalGlobal does not endorse products or services in order to maintain corporate neutrality. But recently, the CEO of TalGlobal has stated publicly that some products are so good and of such high quality that the company should resell those products. Dietz believes reselling a product naturally implies endorsement.

TalGlobal uses customer case studies in its marketing efforts and endeavors to encourage advocates to participate in customer case studies. But at the same time, the company does not necessarily believe there is an obligation to its vendors to provide case studies about their products and services. According to Dietz, this is not a case of "Do unto others." It is just business.

Dietz confirmed that TalGlobal has allowed employees to speak on behalf of a vendor's interest when the employee was paid as a speaker or contributor. Dietz explained although paid endorsements are allowed at TalGlobal, the statements must remain generic so they run into fewer problems with clearance from within the company. He gives a salient example:

"'International travel can be very dangerous. We believe clients who go to potentially dangerous areas need to have a variety of ways to communicate in an emergency.' That statement would be okay. If you wanted somebody at TalGlobal to say: 'If you're traveling, you need the ABC Corp. security sweep communicator.'—that would probably not be okay unless TalGlobal were reselling the product. In that case, the company would need to disclose the invested interest."

Dietz formerly worked at Giga Information Group, where he spoke to different vendors who wanted him to provide quotations for their press releases regarding their products or services. He remembers the policy of Gideon I. Gartner, Giga's CEO, "If you want to talk to my analysts, you have to pay for it." In other words, Giga followed the "pay-to-say" advocacy model. Some analyst companies believe this philosophy allowed them to remain neutral as market research firms and perhaps stimulated more business on their behalf. There is an inherent paradox, however. Vendors and customers would need to pay for any contribution from the Giga analysts. However, Giga wanted and valued free positive quotes provided by their "press release writing" customers. Giga valued customer recommendations and testimonials about the value Giga provided to them.

And the Paradox Continues...

Another point of view comes from the vice president of corporate marketing and communications for Gridstore, Inc., Douglas Gruehl. According to Gruehl, corporate marketing people generally like to step away and deny an endorsement of any tool used by an employee (depending on the focus of the endorsement). "If they were asking if the employee or company used the tool, I probably would approve it. If they were asking how the employee or company were leveraging it for a competitive advantage, I would disapprove it. A benign

endorsement helps them while causing no detriment to me. However, if they were asking us how we were using the tool, when we used
it, why we used it, then the company is starting to expose the competitive advantage it has, whether it be perceived or real." Protecting the
company and brand is his job.

Gruehl says generally, outside of the executive team and certain senior members, nobody at Gridstore, Inc., has been trained to
understand the nuances of media- or marketing-related questions,
how to stay on message, and what value propositions the company
wants repeated to the market. He says the company wants employees
to tweet and Facebook about value propositions. Thus, Gruehl comments, many employees do not understand the subtle nuances and
pitfalls of public statements or interviews such as "Don't fill the void"
and, therefore, doesn't want employees serving as advocates without
some education and company control of their statements. Although
Gruehl recognizes the paradigm that Gridstore uses customer testimonials, case studies, and press releases with its customers, he states
the company does not completely prevent employees from doing the
same for vendors but suggests that employee endorsements and comments must be controlled, reviewed, and managed. In many cases,
employees may only be allowed to validate that they are using a
specific tool or application and not provide details beyond that. He
tries to be flexible, but it is his job to protect the company. Gridstore
embraces the old paradigm of relationship building while taking steps
to protect its brand.

You Are Not Paranoid. They Are Watching You.

Lately, an increasing number of companies are becoming proactive in managing and monitoring employees' opinions and photos on social media. They check social media sites before making

employment offers to job applicants. They check employee activities and advocacies for anything and everything that may affect the company brand. Although companies encourage employees to advocate for the company's products and services and issues the company cares about, they do so cautiously.

One example of a company checking on an employee's advocacy efforts comes from a writer who was hired by a West Coast software company. He was hired to write Web content and develop a media relations strategy to increase product visibility for the environmental software company. Before joining the company, the writer coordinated social media activities and writing content, including content for corporate blogs. He also penned his own blog that featured perspectives on environmental issues.

Several months after he was hired, he was informed by a company official that only authorized personnel within the company were allowed to publicly comment on issues relevant to its business. The content provider did not realize when he took the position that he would be giving up his personal blog so he could avoid running afoul of company policies and issues. The writer agreed to discontinue writing his personal blog advocating about environmental issues to comply with the company policy. This example illustrates the opening assertion in this chapter: Most businesses are autocracies.

Highlights and Takeaways

The following are a few highlights and takeaways from this chapter:

- Some industries are regulated and specifically prohibited from any testimonials concerning the investment adviser or any advice, analysis, report, or other service rendered by such investment adviser.

- Due to the multiple marketing channels today, it is not practical for companies to think they can restrict employees from serving as advocates for a brand or cause.

- A company's restrictive policy may restrict an employee's right to free speech but may not (in practice) prevent the employee from representing the company that endorses a product or service.

- Companies are becoming more proactive at managing and monitoring employees' opinions and social media activities for anything that may affect the company brand.

- There is always a level of risk to an advocate who takes a stand.

About Larry Dietz

Larry Dietz' background combines commercial and military experience. He is an insightful senior executive with a broad background in market intelligence, customer support, and legal matters, with exceptional international exposure at the highest levels. He has peerless strategic planning and business development talents. Dietz is a licensed attorney with emphasis on complex business transactions that involve international partners, contracts, and intellectual property issues. He is a retired U.S. Army Reserve Colonel who supported pandemic influenza planning and operations, is fully fluent in the Federal Emergency Management Agency's (FEMA's) National Information Management Systems (NIMS), and has served as a Department of Defense consultant for Information Operations and Psychological Operations (PSYOP). He is an extraordinary communicator, mentor, and team builder. He has a bachelor of science degree in business administration, a juris doctor, a master of business administration, and master's degrees in strategic studies and in European Union law. Dietz is a member of the bars of the Supreme Court of the United

States and of the state of California. He publishes his blog on psychological operations at www.psyopregiment.blogspot.com.

About Douglas W. Gruehl

Douglas Gruehl is a highly skilled corporate communications and
marketing professional with extensive career history in global branding, corporate strategy, events, global public relations and strategic
marketing communications, and analyst relations. His area of focus
has been in the high-technology field working with some of the major
players in Silicon Valley, including Amdahl, Fujitsu, LEGATO, and
EMC, where he leads international cross-functional marketing teams
dispersed across five continents. Early in his career, he was part of
the marketing team that launched the first Apple Macintosh, Steve
Jobs' NEXT Cube, and the market's first laptop, the WorkSlate. In
addition to his high-tech career, Gruehl is a nationally award-winning
California Community Colleges instructor in the fields of marketing
and merchandising. He has a bachelor of arts degree in liberal and
performing arts.

Doug Is an Advocate

"Personally, I am a huge fan/advocate for the Jaguar brand of cars.
Their attention to detail in their styling and finishes carries on the
legacy traditions of refined elegance of this storied brand. The driving
experience, from the road handling to the interior creature comforts,
provides a level of luxury that cannot be matched by any of the other
brands. They have maintained their exclusivity with their limited
model selection so you don't see yourself coming and going. I try to
persuade anyone buying a car to only consider Jaguar—bar none, the
best cars I have ever owned."

14

Survey Says: Engage Your Advocates as Partners at Every Opportunity

One of the oldest forms of engaging customers is through a traditional survey. Conducting a survey is simple enough: Ask questions, record answers, analyze the responses, and report the results. Every day, we conduct surveys without thinking when we ask our family and friends, "How are you doing? How are you feeling today? What's on your mind?"

Who came up with the first survey? No one is really sure, but we know that ancient Roman emperors polled their citizens in the form of census surveys, and this practice has continued for thousands of years. During the Middle Ages, respondents were typically local authorities such as the clergy who reported on the numbers and the occupations of their parishioners. Far beyond the census, the survey continues to be a common and useful tool today to identify and predict trends, preferences, and behaviors. The results influence many, many aspects of our daily lives from predicting how we will vote (and moving funding accordingly) to designing the products we use.

As marketers, we generally talk about surveying as a research tool. The survey tool has been used for a census, interview, evaluation, litmus test for satisfaction, and ideation. Discussions usually focus on the process of collecting data to support a strategic objective or test market acceptance for a product or service. But for Dr. Pamela Kiecker Royall, head of research at Royall & Company,[1] surveys are more than a research tool. Surveying also offers her a way to build and manage relationships with clients and her targeted audience by engaging and deepening relationships with advocates to gather the voice of the customer (VOC).

Elevating research from a tactical tool to a relationship-building strategy is a key differentiator for Royall & Company, a Virginia-based direct marketing firm that works with colleges and universities on student recruitment and advancement programs. Using data-proven research as part of its relationship-building strategy has positioned Royall & Company as an influential market leader with a client list of several hundred institutions within the higher-education sector.

Royall & Company was founded in 1983 as a direct response venture to serve major national nonprofit organizations. After a single successful engagement with one college client, the firm leveraged customer referrals to grow the company's higher-education business. Building advocates and activating the voice of the consumer has resulted in tremendous growth for Royall & Company. The company now enjoys relationships with many private and state universities, Ivy League schools, small Christian colleges, and single-gender institutions—schools across the nation in which enrollment trends vary widely in student needs and goals, region, student demographics, and backgrounds. The company has combined traditional client satisfaction research methods with innovative advocacy strategies to improve engagement between its client-facing team members and institutional partners.

Relationships can be deepened through survey research because a survey instrument does more than just collect data. Recognizing this fact, Dr. Kiecker Royall believes that a skillfully designed and targeted survey can be a key differentiator in research design and analysis. It drives researchers to more closely monitor the messages conveyed in the interactions between researchers (your business) and respondents (your customers). Factors such as the tone and structure of a survey—how a researcher invites respondents to participate in a study, how the specific questions are structured—represent the voice of the firm. Kiecker Royall reports respondents come away from a survey experience with an impression of the maturity and integrity of the sponsoring institution and its attitude toward its clients. Its influence on the client-stakeholder relationship is profound.

Royall & Company also leverages advocate marketing strategies to enhance relationships with key decision makers at colleges and universities while simultaneously advancing its own business development goals. Its rapid concentration of new business in higher education seemed almost organic, starting with organizing the voice of the customer. Royall & Company used its relationship with deans of admissions—a key constituent group—to present powerful testimonials to prospective clients. Compelling testimonials are posted on the company's Web site and are placed in the collateral materials presented at higher-education conferences. Selected administrators' pictures are prominently displayed along with quotations that describe strategic successes and Royall's role in their success. Over time, the program of testimonials and peer advocacy developed momentum as others noted the growth and achievement of Royall & Company's advocate institutions. Soon the opportunity to be a Royall brand advocate became a highly coveted role among academic institutions, a role that has inspired more participation in the program and has driven new business opportunities among prospects. Years later, new partners still inquire about becoming an advocate.

Research Techniques Communicate a Client's Brand and Values

In addition to relationship building, Kiecker Royall regards using surveys as an opportunity to positively influence perceptions of prospective students. For instance, Royall & Company's research team looks for opportunities to advance relationships between its partner institutions and prospective students, even when prospective students indicate they will not enroll at the institution. Their forward-thinking strategy considers the possibility of other future engagements. Although students may not enroll now, the recruitment process should leave them with a positive view of the institution, leaving open the possibilities for the future. Students could consider enrolling as graduate students, or become candidates for future employment at the school. Their grown children might consider enrolling at the school in the future. In other words, all communications during the initial student recruitment process play a role in building opinions about the school, its brand, and values.

Conducting surveys is a real challenge to researchers to ensure that it accurately reflects the client's brand and values to respondents, according to Kiecker Royall. When well designed and delivered, surveys are an "open door" for respondents to share their thoughts about the organization. When the survey functions as an invitation to provide feedback, including constructive criticism, you can uncover the voice of the customer. These critical but sometimes nuanced insights can be used to guide future communication plans and growth strategies. And this can translate into solid and sustainable profits for your company.

While surveys are a powerful tool by themselves, their results can complement the findings of focus group research. When recruiting focus group participants, however, care must be taken to assemble the right individuals. Researchers should attempt to learn as much as they can about the demographic, behavioral, and psychological profile of the group in order to tease out important, but credible, insights. If you have a group of only advocates in the room to talk about an organization, you effectively stack the cards in favor of the organization. In other cases, the voice of a single, outspoken advocate (or detractor) can unduly influence the discussion and results of the focus group. Once recruited, however, researchers need to look for signs to tell if they are hearing from advocates, influencers, or detractors when determining the real insights offered by participants' comments.

Royall Partners with Clients to Promote Achievements

Royall & Company conducts several corporate survey projects each year, engaging client institutions as partners in the process. Many survey ideas are generated from a list of "top-interest" topics from the client base. Recent surveys have explored financial considerations of families involved in the college search process and students' communication preferences among themselves, with parents, and with the university. Topics like these are of interest to virtually every institution in Royall & Company's client portfolio and provide the opportunity to share content of the greatest value with clients. These cooperative projects help Royall reach its research goals, and the brainstorming and camaraderie generated from discussions about potential research topics also strengthens client relationships. When Royall's college partners are invited to participate in survey planning and preparation—and given the privilege of early-release findings—they are being treated as an exclusive club member. This often attracts the interest of other clients and prospects, generating more opportunities for greater engagement. In the world of high technology, this would be similar to alpha or beta testers collaborating with a company to make a solution better.

In another effort to leverage the strength of its relationships with partner institutions, Royall & Company engages institutional representatives—university presidents as well as deans of admission—in advocacy roles. When clients achieve ambitious goals, they become "case studies" for others to aspire to match. University representatives join Royall & Company representatives to share their success stories in collaborative materials and/or presentations at conferences attended by many key prospects.

Partnerships Drive High Client Retention Rate

The strength of Royall & Company's brand is best reflected in its client retention rate of 96 percent. That's a big selling point when Royall approaches a prospective client. Kiecker Royall reports that when clients discontinue their relationship with the firm, the decision is almost always driven by fiscal constraints, and not dissatisfaction. And in many cases, Kiecker Royall says, clients return after a brief hiatus, recognizing that the financial investment is necessary to their institutional health and well-being. Royall team members always part on friendly terms with clients. In fact, Royall continues to share some research resources even when the service agreements have expired.

Clients also maintain their engagement after formal service agreements lapse, too. When one former client noticed his testimonial was no longer included on the Royall & Company Web site, he called to ask what had happened. It was his sincere desire to have his endorsement retained and asked that it be included on the Web site. The message was clear: He was committed to recommending Royall to colleagues.

Despite its success, Royall does not rest on its solid reputation. Its innovative team constantly tests new technologies and tactics, including SMS and IM channels, Facebook integration, and mobile-optimized campaigns. These strategies and others ensure its place as a major marketing player in higher education.

Highlights and Takeaways

The following are a few highlights and takeaways from this chapter:

- Surveys are the original engagement tool. Use them to your advantage with your advocates to engage as often as possible without being a nuisance.

- Surveys are an excellent tool to promote clients' brand image and deepen relationships as well as collect data for market research.

- A toolkit of advocate marketing tactics, such as promoting university administrators' endorsements at leading higher-education conferences, drive prospects' interest in becoming clients and advocates.

About Dr. Pamela Kiecker Royall

Dr. Pamela Kiecker Royall leads Royall & Company's efforts to survey prospective students, enrolled students, and alumni, as well as parents, high school counselors, admission professionals, and other key stakeholders. Her higher-education experience spans more than twenty years as a university faculty member and administrator. Pam holds a PhD in business administration from the University of Colorado at Boulder, an MBA from Minnesota State University, Mankato, and a BA from Carleton College. She currently serves as a trustee of Carleton College and is chair of the advisory board of Massey Cancer Center at Virginia Commonwealth University. The customized research programs that Kiecker Royall heads at Royall provide information to guide strategic planning and decision making for its higher-education clients in both enrollment management and advancement.

Pam Is an Advocate

"My behavior says I'm a fan of Starbucks. I go to Starbucks every day and yet, I've never had a cup of coffee in my life! I go to Starbucks for hot tea, which is not their standard offering. I put hundreds of dollars on my mobile app and I suggest to colleagues that we meet at Starbucks. When I visit with my ninety-seven-year-old mother-in-law, I always bring her a Starbucks' latte and morning bun. Yet, as a marketing professional, I recognize the limitations with the company's service format. I wait in line. And I tolerate 'out-of-stock' situations when my favorite tea is not available. And I clean up the mess that the last guest left behind. Despite all its flaws, I certainly am a fan. And a non-coffee drinker, at that!"

Endnote

1. In interest of full disclosure, the author is a former student and client. She continues to maintain a professional relationship with Dr. Kiecker Royall and is an advocate for Royall & Company's research services.

15

Advocates Turning Rogue: The Importance of Reputation Management

Imagine you are driving home after a hard day's work. It's about dinnertime and you are getting hungry. You push a button on your steering wheel and say, "Siri, what's the best Italian restaurant near me?"

"OK," she says in her female, intelligent assistant, natural tone. "One of these Italian restaurants looks fairly close to you. I've sorted them by rating."

The first question that should pop up into your mind is, "Whose rating?" iPhone doesn't collect ratings for restaurants. You haven't loaded ratings of your favorite restaurants into your phone.

The answer is Yelp's ratings. During Apple's 2011 "Let's Talk iPhone" event, keynote speaker, Scott Forstall, former senior vice president of iOS software at Apple, Inc., stated that Apple had formed a partnership with Yelp. Under this agreement, the technology giant has integrated Yelp's rankings into the iOS system's processes for sorting restaurants.[1] That's how Siri sorts restaurants when you ask for searches of nearby "best" restaurants on iOS 4S.

The Importance of User Feedback

Although most forms of advocate marketing tactics are growing in popularity, none match the meteoric rise of online reviews. Customer reviews are playing a bigger role as big data feeds search engine algorithms, and reviews are becoming a more trusted source of information when making purchasing decisions.

Although this trend is helping consumers make informed choices about local services, scammers and criminals are leveraging online review sites, looking for opportunities to defraud or defame. Getting a false or malicious review removed from an online review site can be extremely difficult. Sites such as TripAdvisor, Yelp, and Angie's List often refuse to remove negative reviews without a court injunction. When brands are under attack or reputations are damaged online, organizations turn to experts such as Steven Wyer, chief executive of Third Coast Interactive, a digital marketing firm based in Nashville, Tennessee.

Embracing Online Reviews

In a survey conducted by BrightLocal,[2] 85 percent of consumers indicated they read online reviews for information regarding local businesses.[3] This is part of an emerging trend as consumers leverage the wealth of consumer-generated information to research local and international products and services before making buying decisions.

Social media has empowered consumers with a full spectrum of online review tools such as Yelp, TripAdvisor, Google+ Local, OpenTable, and Foursquare, whose growing popularity are driving increased interest in online feedback. In response, businesses are scrambling to develop new engagement strategies to take advantage of positive reviews for growth and competitive benefits. However, just as advocates go public with positive reviews that encourage product or service purchases, so are detractors with negative reviews that deter or extinguish purchasing decisions.

New Technology Boosts Reviews

When was the last time you provided a review of a product or service? Was it a positive or negative review? A recent infograph[4] compiled by Dr. William Ward of www.dr4ward.com features data points indicating that 75 percent of customer reviews online are positive. Another data point highlights the fact that 82 percent of consumers consider reviews to be valuable. In addition, 83 percent of respondents said they would trust a user's review over a critic's review. According to Wyer, potential buyers now consider online reviews to be a viable source of information when selecting service providers such as restaurants, real estate agents, doctors and dentists, hotels, electricians, plumbers, and more.

Favorable online ratings are important to advance a business's competitive standing. A study by Harvard Business School[5] indicated that a one-star rating bump can increase revenues between 5 and 9 percent for a restaurant listed on Yelp.

Do consumers trust these sites to provide fair assessments of local businesses? In "Customer Rating and Reviews Site: An Upcoming Crisis of Confidence,"[6] David Ensing of Maritz Research looked into consumers' opinions of online reviews and concluded:

> *"Seventy-five percent of consumers think that the information presented in review sites is generally fair. These people do admit, though, that consumers need to discern for themselves the level of trustworthiness of the user-generated reviews and ratings that they read. Meanwhile, 16 percent of respondents believe that review sites are overly negative, while 9 percent think they are overly positive."*

However, a recent article in *Time* magazine[7] now casts doubt on processes used to manage some consumer review Web sites. It cites a study by *Consumer Reports* that investigated the practices of popular online review sites, including Yelp and Angie's List, as well as lesser-known firms such as Porch. The study "calls into question the validity and trustworthiness of user-review sites. Unsettling surprises came fast and frequently." It states:

> "Angie's List, which only allows its two million paying subscribers to see (and write) local business reviews, is criticized due to its practice of allowing businesses with a B rating or better to pay to get their listing placed at the top of search results. 'We think that the ability of A- and B-rated companies to buy their way to the top of the default search results skews the results...' CR researchers write. 'Angie's List misleads consumers by prominently promising that "businesses don't pay" and that it's a consumer-driven service supported by membership fees. But almost 70 percent of the company's revenues come from advertising purchased by the service providers being rated.'"

Tuttle continues, offering that Google+ Local's ratings are similarly questionable because ratings can be skewed as customers are cajoled into posting more-flattering reviews or deleting less-favorable ones. Yelp's ratings also tend to skew high—66 percent of the first quarter of 2013's reviews were four or five stars—and Yelp correlates this to high and repeat usage. In other words, the more movies, for example, a person rents, the more likely she is to post a positive review.[8] Tuttle warns his readers that, in line with the old maxim, just because someone says something online does not mean that it's true. The wise individual or business owner digs deeper to find out what is really behind those assessments when her reputation is on the line.

Encouraging Positive Online Reviews

According to Wyer, businesses are becoming aware of two important challenges associated with online reviews:

- **They need to develop strategies that encourage satisfied customers to post online reviews**—More than 80 percent of people who have a bad customer experience will go online and post a review, according to Marketing Pilgrim's Frank Reed.[9] Vitals.com, a Web site that provides referrals to medical professionals, reported 73 percent growth in 2013.[10] The Web site had 1.5 million unique visitors to the site looking for a physician referral. However, while 50 percent of the people looking for a doctor read online reviews, less than 1 in 10 ever file a review themselves.

- **Seventy-four percent of consumers refuse to interact or do business with a person or company that has negative information published about them online.**[11]—Negative reviews have a powerful impact on purchasing decisions. Affected companies need to act quickly to generate favorable feedback that provides a balanced view of their customers' opinions. Other strategies to offset negative reviews can include conducting their own customer satisfaction surveys and sharing customer testimonials publicly when given permission. Other key performance indicators of customer success and satisfaction include a high referral rate or Net Promoter Score (NPS), a high renewal rate, or customer satisfaction rate.

Businesses Generate Favorable Reviews

Many organizations find themselves at a disadvantage because their specific business focus areas do not easily accommodate requests for online reviews. On their own, customers are relieved that their service request has been addressed, but tend to remain silent once the work is completed. Surprisingly, companies have found that when specifically asked, many satisfied customers are enthusiastic about providing an endorsement after a favorable experience. With a growing number of consumers making decisions based on online reviews, favorable reviews are needed in order to remain competitive and this takes deliberately reaching out to the customer base, which costs company time, money, and effort.

To help companies generate more positive reviews, technology firms have introduced powerful software tools such as The Review Solution. This application, built in partnership with the Better Business Bureau (BBB), makes it simple and efficient for small businesses to request reviews from their customers at the point of service. The Review Solution forwards a request from a service provider for consumers to rate their experience and seamlessly forwards the information for use in an online review.

Elsewhere, the BBB, an institution that has documented consumer complaints since 1912, recently recognized the value of allowing consumers to report excellent service as well as complaints. Locally focused, about 40 percent of local BBB offices now accept positive customer feedback and post those comments to their Web sites. BBB officials are considering expanding the program nationwide.

In addition, several companies, such as McDonald's fast-food restaurants, use the purchase receipt to encourage guests to visit a Web site to complete a customer satisfaction survey. The feedback is shared directly with the restaurant to help make the guest's next visit an excellent experience. If it appears that the quality of the service experience did not meet expectations, the guest has the option to request a direct contact from the restaurant to resolve the concerns.

Claiming Your Online Identity

Wyer provides a stark reality check when asked about online threats to a company's brand or an individual's reputation. He warns that failing to properly manage a virtual identity opens the door to shadowy figures—trolls, as they are sometimes called—who obtain online identities to defame or defraud others. Reputation management experts like Wyer say the best way to avoid online fraud is to establish and self-manage online identities on LinkedIn, Facebook, Twitter, Pinterest, Google+, and other major social platforms—even if there is no intention to activate those accounts.

Wyer also advises that individuals and companies visit a Web domain registrar, such as GoDaddy or Network Solutions, and enter the individual's name or business title to find out whether it is available or has been purchased by someone else. If it is available, consider acquiring it as soon as possible. It is critical to check every possible permutation of the name, including FirstNameLastName, FirstNameMiddleNameLastName, FirstNameMiddleInitialLastName, CompanyName, CompanyNameAbbreviation, CompanyNameLocation, etc., and by the different URL extensions, such as *.com*, *.net*, *.mil*, *.gov*, *.us*, *.biz*, etc. By not owning those identities, a rogue detractor can buy them and can put any type of content on that Web site. At that point, halting or mitigating fraudulent activity is extremely difficult (if not impossible) and expensive. Wyer even suggests that parents obtain domains and URLs for their newborns to ensure a child's identity isn't compromised before she begins kindergarten.

An incident involving one of Wyer's clients provides a chilling illustration of how trolls can use social platforms to damage a brand or individual's reputation. The client was a retired firefighter who wrote a popular weekly newspaper column in a small New England town. One particular column took an unpopular stand on a volatile political issue. Persons taking the opposite view of that issue became enraged and decided to use an online forum to attack the columnist. They bought a domain with the columnist's name embedded and effectively took virtual control of his online identity. The group launched a well-orchestrated effort to build a Web site and populate it with highly defamatory content while carefully concealing their own identities. Unable to stop the deluge of insults, Wyer's client watched helplessly as his reputation was ruined in public view. Frustrated and embarrassed, he finally moved out of town.

URLs and social media platforms offer the ability for individuals and organizations to build an identity that aligns with their brand. However, Wyer says claiming and managing a virtual identity across the Web in all social media platforms is just as important as owning an organization's or individual's identity. It is no longer a question of having an identity online. The critical question is just who is controlling that identity?

Selecting a Reputation Management Strategy

Managing a virtual reputation must be part of a business's strategic plan and must contain contingency plans to ensure that the business survives if that reputation is sullied. Wyer warns consumers to be careful when selecting a reputation management firm. Just as there are reputation trolls, there are bad actors that pose as legitimate firms. For instance, a client was desperate for action when he spotted negative comments about his firm in an online review site. He found a Web site that advertised reputation management services and hired the firm by sending a $5,000 cashier's check overnight to the published address. After payment was made, nothing happened and, predictably, nothing was resolved. The client turned to Wyer to research the first company hired and to help repair his online reputation. Tracing the transaction, Wyer found that the check was delivered to a one-bedroom apartment that rented for $350 per month.

Another ploy used by people posing as reputation management experts is to go to Web sites such as RipOffReport.com that offer anonymous postings. They are commonly used because users do not have to verify the validity of their complaints. RipOffReport.com, which claims to have 1.7 million complaints posted, generates such a high volume of activity that it garners high search engine optimization (SEO) ratings. According to Wyer, trolls can use that to their advantage by posting multiple false claims online. They then approach the affected business, point out the citations, and offer to clear the postings for a substantial fee.

Wyer says reputation management firms support advocate marketing by educating individuals and organizations about the risks to their brands when free access to information and easy publication platforms converge. People contact him when they feel helpless because they don't understand why their identity was co-opted or, significantly, how this occurred on the Internet, an often mysterious territory. He has observed that when consumers better understand what has happened to them and why, they are less likely to become victims again, and they are better equipped to develop a response.

Highlights and Takeaways

The following are a few highlights and takeaways from this chapter:

- Businesses should monitor their online reputation and check for negative reviews or complaints.

- Customers with negative experiences are more likely to post a review online than those with positive experiences.

- The use and importance of online consumer reviews are expanding rapidly as consumers use data to make decisions.

- Businesses are developing innovative strategies to encourage customers to post reviews online.

- Companies and individuals should take proactive steps to prevent online reputation damage by claiming domains that have the individuals' names or business titles before detractors can use them for defamation.

- Reputation management services can provide guidance and online reputation restoration if a virtual identity has been deliberately damaged.

About Steven Wyer

Steven Wyer serves as chief executive of Third Coast Interactive. The firm provides online reputation management, online review management, and consulting services.

He has been a consultant to financial institutions involved in consumer lending and collections, mortgage lending, and institutional asset management. He is affiliated with several professional organizations, including the National Association of Securities Dealers, the Mortgage Bankers Association, the Direct Marketing Association, American Teleservices Association, the Debt Buyers Association, and the eMarketing Association.

Wyer is the author of *Violated Online*, a book that chronicles the issues that clients have faced as victims of online slander, damaging online reviews, and virtual identity misuse. He also serves on the Advisory Board of the Middle Tennessee Better Business Bureau.

Wyer resides in Franklin, Tennessee, with his wife, children, and creatures.

Steven Is an Advocate

"I'm an advocate for Apple. Why am I an advocate for Apple? Because they have truly gone to the source of need and provided a solution. I don't ever have to come up with a workaround when I use their product. I just use the product. There are many brands, but if I were going to be a cheerleader for a brand, certainly Apple would be right up there at the top. In addition, Whole Foods does a great job. Publix also is an amazing, amazing grocery store. They offer a wonderful level of customer service and attentiveness. It is materially different from other stores. If I were going to stick three bumper stickers on my car, they would be for Apple, Whole Foods, and Publix."

Endnotes

1. Scott Forstall, "Let's Talk iPhone," October 11, 2011, http://events.apple.com. edgesuite.net/11piuhbvdlbkvoih10/event/index.html.

2. Myles Anderson, "Welcome to Findings of the BrightLocal Local Consumer Review Survey 2013," BrightLocal, 2012.

3. Jennifer Slegg, "Local Business Reviews Read by 85% of Consumers," Search Engine Watch, June 2013.

4. Dr. William Ward, "Dr.4Ward," http://www.dr4ward.com/dr4ward/2013/03/what-are-some-interesting-statistics-about-online-consumer-reviews-infographic. html.

5. Michael Luca, "Reviews, Reputation, and Revenue: The Case of Yelp.com," 2011, http://www.hbs.edu/faculty/Publication%20Files/12-016_0464f20e-35b2-492e-a328-fb14a325f718.pdf.

6. David Ensing, "Customer Rating and Reviews Site: An Upcoming Crisis of Confidence?" Maritz Research, 2013, http://www.reviewtrackers.com/75-percent-consumers-online-reviews-ratings-fair/.

7. Brad Tuttle, "Guess Who's Getting Some Awful Reviews: User Review Sites," *Time*, September 2013, http://business.time.com/2013/09/21/guess-whos-getting-some-pretty-awful-reviews-user-review-sites/.

8. Ibid.

9. Frank Reed, "Eighty Percent of Shoppers Change Purchase Decision Based on Negative Decision Marketing," Pilgrim, August 2011.

10. Review Trackers, "Eighty-Two Percent of Patients Say Online Reviews Influence Willingness to Be Treated by a Doctor," November 2013, http://www.reviewtrackers.com/82-percent-patients-online-reviews-influence-willingness-treated-doctor/.

11. Joy Hawkins, "Relevance and Impact of Online Reviews," Imprezzio Marketing, 2014.

16

Best Practices for Creating a Project Management Plan for an Advocate Recognition Engagement (ARE) Program

The previous chapter shares the story of how the Advocate Recognition Engagement (ARE) program came to fruition. This chapter expands on the steps described in the previous case study and provides more specific advice to create a sustainable program.

Once you have determined critical roles and responsibilities (from managers to staff workers to outside consultants and vendors), create your strategic plan. This plan outlines timelines, budgets, tools and technologies needed, and your specific goals and how they will be measured. Table 16.1 provides an example of a simple project management chart. It identifies the key stages of the project and the steps to consider.

Table 16.1 A Sample Project Plan

Components	Activities	Status	Tools	Due Date	Start Date	Budget	KPI	Approved
Planning	Roles and responsibilities							
Planning	Strategic marketing plan							
Planning	Timeline/budget							
Planning	Executive endorsement							
Planning	Team roles							
Communications	Internal communication milestones—launch, FAQ, policies and process, updates, etc.							
Communications	External communication milestones—Web, e-mails, FAQ, forms, etc.							
Launch	Internal launch to educate teams and gather list of nominees							
Launch	External launch to engage nominees—e-mails, calls, entry forms							
Launch	Sponsor campaign to engage media and partners, news release or media alert, e-mails, calls							
Media/Partner Sponsor Campaign	Bartered or paid agreement, sponsor materials for pre, during, and post award event, etc.							

Components	Activities	Status	Tools	Due Date	Start Date	Budget	KPI	Approved
Nominee Campaign	Master list of nominees, e-mails, calls, entry forms							
Nominee Entry Case Studies	Interview, draft, editors, approvals, judges evaluations, final content products							
Awards and Ceremony	Notifications to internal teams and winners, gifts, guidelines, public announcements, engravings, photos, videos, posting stories, pitching stories, VIP treatments, award presentation, script, souvenir event booklet, case study booklet, hotel contract, award show details							
Post-Event	Posting and pitching content, thank-you notes, production of video, communications of where content is posted to internal and external people							
Analytics	Profile winners, evaluate feedback from event, gather accounts from internal/external people, how engaged was the winner and their company, media pickups and impressions and results of the goals set in the planning stages							

Using this table as a model, your team should be able to develop a strong project management tool because you have captured the information that is vital for success.

Through *your* ARE, you are creating not just an award but a sustainable award program. Figure 16.1 outlines the stages involved, based on the ARE program.

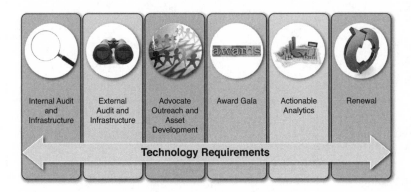

Figure 16.1 Stages of a continuous ARE program

As you can see, technology is the foundation of the program supporting all of the stages of the ARE program. Having the right technology that supports the entire process is vital for analytics and provides your executive sponsor with the evidence he needs to justify the renewal of this program. Using the right technologies saves you time, performs status analysis, and provides you with a minute-by-minute snapshot of your program data so you can identify program risks and points that merit more focus. This list of the technology capabilities is worth considering as you develop your program:

- CRM solution
- Lead nurturing solution with survey and e-mailing capabilities
- Social media management solution
- An analytics or SEO metrics management solution

If you do not have these tools or access to them or budget for them, consider free technology that might be available to fill these needs.

Project Management Stages

Let's examine these stages more thoroughly.

Internal Audit and Infrastructure Stage

In the Internal Audit and Infrastructure stage, you are setting up your foundation. Goals are established. You identify what is needed, what needs to be created, who is needed, who is involved, and which forms and templates are needed. The program's policies and standards are produced, and the scope for the number of awards and categories is determined. Award categories are defined but should be *very* flexible to maximize participation.

This stage may include creating (or drafting) materials for the following:

- Communications and frequency
- Training
- Toolkits and templates
- Timelines and schedules for goals
- Internal Web pages

During this stage, you begin outreach within your organization, including the following:

- Involving business lines, customer care, sales, product management, and other internal staff
- Sharing your budget with departments
- Identifying external resources, including partners

The tools, processes, strategies, and technologies you use for advocate marketing are very much the same you use for integrated marketing. If your advocate is willing to engage in tweeting or retweeting (for example), you need the tools, processes, strategies, and technology to identify, assess, manage, and analyze her activity and the value that activity provides to your company. Advocate marketing infrastructure may include leveraging resources you already have within your organization. If those people or solutions are limited, new, additional people and technology may be needed.

External Audit and Infrastructure Stage

In the External Audit and Infrastructure stage, you prepare to open the doors and windows to the public: what happens when, who does what, how to answer customer questions, and how to contact the customers to get them involved and engaged.

This stage may include creating and implementing many outreach tasks:

- Create briefs of the promotions
- Set external Web pages
- Build toolkits and templates for FAQ, entry form, rules, and guidelines
- Provide training to communicate each external step
- Identify timelines to guide and track
- Create the press release to canvas nominations
- Craft pitch to customers
- Identify and confirm sponsors
- Execute the social media strategy and plans
- Create the award icon and guidelines (press kit for winners)
- Get creative input needed for award program design

- Create final list of nominees
- Schedule the event gala scheduled and book the venue
- Purchase the awards
- Design and put together the gift baskets and award announcements

Advocate Outreach and Asset Development Stage

In the Advocate Outreach and Asset Development stage, content flows, such as press releases dropping, social media tweets, e-mails going out, postings on sites appearing, and calls being made to gather entries for creating case studies. No case study is started until a signed rules form is collected.

This stage includes the following:

- Schedule and carry out interviews with nominees
- Write interview questions for each customer
- Communicate progress and status to internal teams
- Conduct interviews with internal and external contacts
- Transcribe interviews
- Write case studies, confirm layout, get written final approvals
- Notify internal teams of finalized case studies
- Send out gift baskets and award announcements
- Write and send out press release listing all winners
- Pitch stories to publications before public

Award Gala Stage

The Award Gala stage is one of the most enjoyable parts of this program. Understandably, this is the most vital stage. It is what your advocates love most—they get public appreciation. Appreciation is the key to the magical chemistry felt by an advocate. There are three basic components of showing appreciation:

- Praise
- Recognition
- Reward

This stage may include creating materials for the following:

- Event gala presentation slides
- Event gala script
- Music selected
- Web pages set up and content updated
- Toolkits and templates
- Internal communication and training
- Social media strategy and plans
- Event gala production and direction

Of course, you need staff to stage and support every task in the actual event.

Actionable Analytics Stage

The Actionable Analytics stage is where you measure what you have managed and manage what you have measured. Here the loop is closed and the success you were able to attain through the program becomes evident. The goals that were set in the internal audit stage are brought forward and your key performance indicators are measured against those goals.

This stage may include the following:

- Create the final report on news release pickups and coverage
- Social media coverage—tweets and retweets
- Track customer postings on award and recognition Web pages
- Facilitate customer participation in news releases, tweets, and other social media
- Write profiles of participating advocates, capturing such information as company revenue to date, description of the company (e.g., Fortune 500 or Global 500 company), industry, and other demographics

Renewal Stage

In the Renewal stage, you create your presentation to the executive team to justify repeating the program. Ask to meet with the executive team to share your findings. Align your presentation to the corporate strategy goals and provide two to three results as value proof points per goal. Work with your executive sponsor to hone the messaging of this final presentation to seal the renewal. And like a good sales representative should always do, ask for the renewal at the end of your presentation.

Highlights and Takeaways

The following are a few highlights and takeaways from this chapter:

- Secure an executive sponsor that is 100 percent supportive to your project.

- Create the strategic plan outlining strategy, policies and process, timelines, resources and budgets, tools and technology, and goals.

- Break down the project into stages with milestones identified in each stage.

- Get the evidence you need to present to the executive team so your project is renewed and financially supported.

17

Best Practices in the B2B Customer Advocacy and Reference Industry

SiriusDecisions first launched its Customer Advocacy and Engagement Survey back in 2013. Its 2015 version continues its successful format, while adding a few new questions that target marketing professionals. From this survey, SiriusDecisions created the *State of B-to-B Customer Advocacy* and *2015 Reference Report*. Currently, it is the only industry report that covers this topic. In 2015, more than 200 companies participated in the survey.

During an address at the 2015 Summit on Customer Engagement, Megan Heuer, vice president at SiriusDecisions, told the audience that customer advocacy is the future of marketing. When Heuer shared some results from the *State of B-to-B Customer Advocacy* and *2015 Reference Report*, one thing was very clear: The report's conclusions are truer today than ever before. When customer advocacy professionals or customer reference professionals think about what they do, it is all about how to get customers to be advocates. Heuer said she believes that putting customers at the center is what defines a company's business value.

Heuer started her session by defining a few terms as part of her research and presentation:

- *Customer experience* is defined as the experience a customer has with your brand. Customer experience includes both your buyer's journey and your post-sale customer life cycle. Customer experience is the umbrella.

- *Customer advocacy* is underneath that umbrella as a collection of interactions and opportunities for customers to engage with you.

- A *customer advocate* is someone who is willing to speak on your behalf, formally or informally, via rumor or via a very formal case study or via presenting at a conference.

- A *customer reference* is a subset of customer advocates referring to a more traditional sales reference.

What Can Marketers Learn from the Survey?

SiriusDecisions learned that a lot of people really care about this topic. The great news is that the survey reported that 85 percent of advocacy professionals described their role as more than just customer references. Organizations have come to embrace advocacy as a bigger category, and it is becoming more strategic in their company. It is starting to get a seat at the table more often than not. More companies than ever before are expanding their view of customer advocacy. This result is up 26 percent compared with 2013 responses.

According to Heuer, more and more organizations are building direct relationships. They are doing direct outreach to customers. They no longer depend solely on sales and have since reduced sales contests. They use various channels such as surveys and social media to engage with people who are natural advocates.

She told marketing executives that more companies are taking advantage of technology to help them with their advocacy efforts. Technology helps companies scale their marketing efforts. But the best thing about technology now is that there are generalist tools—such as sales for automation, marketing automation—that can be used in the service of advocacy. In addition, there are more dedicated solutions, too. Companies are adopting these technologies to do more with their advocacy efforts and teams.

Heuer said 53 percent of all responders to the SiriusDecisions survey reported that they are looking to invest in technology within the next 12 months. Sixty percent were planning to invest in CRM/Salesforce automation solutions while 44 percent were looking at customer reference platforms, followed by 37 percent who were considering marketing automation platforms. The list of different types of technologies that companies were planning to invest in was long and varied. Advocacy is an incredibly innovative category within technology right now. Technology for advocacy is one area we should all care about, Heuer stressed, because it helps everyone do their job that much better.

According to the report, responders say they plan to spend their 2015 technology investments in the following areas: 54 percent are investing in a customer reference platform, 25 percent are investing in an advocate marketing/gamification platform, 21 percent are investing in an online community platform, tying with 21 percent investing in a marketing automation platform.

Heuer said she sees these as positive signs that companies are realizing the value of advocate marketing. However, as an analyst, she said she always has to look at the dark side of situations. There are a few areas where things may not be where we would like them to be, and companies have an incredible opportunity to do more and do better:

- **Opportunity 1: Sales team members**—Heuer reminded marketers that advocate marketing is still a volunteer army. Seven percent of surveyed companies said sales has customer advocacy as an action item and they are measured on it, which is a less-than-desirable outcome. Advocacy is the lifeblood of your business. Heuer emphasized that if it is voluntary for sales to identify individuals who might be willing to participate in the company advocacy program, marketers must find other ways to get participants. She said marketers should work with sales, but not depend on them for identifying advocates.

- **Opportunity 2: "Rock star" advocates**—According to the survey, only 35 percent of companies said they actually look for their best advocates. They look for those people who are most willing to go out and shout from the rooftops how great it is to work with your company and the value that they've gotten from it. This is way too low, Heuer said. For something so easy to do, marketers should all be looking for rock star advocates. It is easy to find out who these people are. Some organizations have informal processes, but shouldn't be leaving this to chance. This should be something that is a meaningful part of an advocate marketing program, to know and nurture and thank and engage those customers who care the most about your business. This is really important.

- **Opportunity 3: Heed the warning signs**—One important disconnect SiriusDecisions continues to see from responders is around customer strategy. Eighty-three percent of respondents to the survey said they felt customer references were either critical or valuable to their sales cycle—as in "can't close business without it." However, SiriusDecisions noted that less than 10 percent of marketing program dollars is going to secure customer advocacy. What surprises Heuer the most is that this is unchanged from 2013. She raised this caution flag before. This is wild under-resourcing of the lifeblood of your business. If you reviewed all the activities done in marketing that touch customers, could it be coordinated better? Could investments be coordinated better? Is what you are investing in an appropriate investment? Is it a relevant investment? Each chief marketing officer (CMO) should think about this and where those investments fit within a customer-centric strategy.

Do You Really Know Your Customers' Experience with Your Company?

Heuer told the audience that marketing and sales teams histori-cally have played the blame game with each other. Marketing claims they are passing over good leads to sales. Stuffing them into the top of the pipeline based on the service level agreements for what market-ing is supposed to bring to sales, but sales can't close the deals. What's wrong with sales? Meanwhile, the sales team claims they do what they can, but they cannot force somebody to buy. The lead was not really warmed up to buy. The issue may not be a sales or marketing issue.

- **Opportunity 4: Put your customer first**—Heuer asks, "What if the silent killer of your sales pipeline is actually your customer experience?" Do you know what you really are delivering to the market? And what do your customers think about their experi-ence with you? Could that be the reason leads are not closing? Is that why your company doesn't have enough advocates? She says part of your customer strategy has to be putting customers first. Discover their experience through feedback and that will help you find more advocates, and every company can do this.

SiriusDecisions continues to analyze data from its Customer Advocacy and Engagement Survey with the persona studies they have developed. According to Heuer, one of the disconnects experts have seen is that much of content created out of advocacy organizations is relegated to the later stages of the buying cycle. But, think back to the silent killer idea just described: Prospects want information from your customers at *all* stages. If your company is not providing rel-evant information to clients earlier in the sales cycle, they will get it themselves from other sources. That means you risk being taken out of that conversation, she warned. This means that you are missing out on what customers want.

Based on results from survey respondents and overlaying the persona of CXO, 89 percent say their perception of a vendor's brand "moderately to significantly" influences the creation of their short list. Heuer said 75 percent say their research is done via personal interactions and viral communication networks. But 80 percent say their final decision is based on their own or others' experience with your company. So let's return to the question about understanding your customers' experience through their buying journey. Eighteen percent of respondents said they know each buyer's journey *extremely* well. They have it mapped out and know who plays a role throughout. That leaves 82 percent of the companies that haven't done the necessary work. Or, if it has been done in another part of the organization, it has not been communicated to the advocacy team. That is not good. If somebody has done the work, one message that should have been loud and clear is how critically important advocacy is to your buyer during all stages. It certainly shows that in Heuer's research.

- **Opportunity 5: Get advocate information in front of sales**—So, what can we do as advocacy teams to anticipate information needs and map to them? If you think about how each of us buys as an individual, what do you go to first? You go to reviews. You go get information. Your buyers follow the same process when considering whether to purchase your product or service. So why not front-load customer evidence (references, testimonials, case studies) to help throughout all stages? The fact that about 25 percent of respondents purposely don't do it at all is very surprising. But by getting customer information to your advocate marketing team, and advocate materials in front of sales, you can make huge improvements in both your sales pipeline and customer experience. It is a major shift in thinking: a shift to invest time to better focus on what your prospects need and when they want it.[1]

In summary, Heuer advised customer advocacy teams to map each buyer's journey and calculate your customer's life cycle. She said these two pieces of information give you the foundation for making advocacy more powerful within your organization. Ask yourself, "What do I need to do, when do I need to do it, and with whom do I need to do it?"

Next, Heuer suggests completing a simple gap analysis. At this point, ask, "What support is needed, at which stage, what do I have, and what do I need today?" This will help you determine where or what you need to invest in to advance your advocacy program's impact on the business.

Lastly, Heuer encouraged marketers to think about a measurement strategy and communications. If you are not sharing what your advocacy team is doing and the impact you see you're having, no one will know it or see it. She suggested that your marketing strategy identify a clear link between your activity and customer engagement and sales outcome, then start communicating it. This will really help you get the credibility you and your team need to ask for more resources that are clearly necessary. This type of information will allow you to make a case for the investment that will help advocacy fulfill its role as the future of marketing and help make your business—and you personally—more successful. We can all agree on these two good outcomes.

Highlights and Takeaways

The following are a few highlights and takeaways from this chapter:

- Putting customers at the center of your marketing strategy defines your company's business value.

- Marketers need to develop more effective programs that empower and encourage account executives to develop advocates from their client contacts.

- Technology investments help marketers more efficiently analyze customer experience data.

Endnote

1. Megan Heuer, presentation at 2015 Summit on Customer Engagement, February 24, 2015.

18 ————————————

Best Practices for Measurability

In today's B2B marketing ecosystem, promotional campaigns alone do not lead to a sale. As companies increase marketing investments, chief marketing officers (CMOs) are facing increased pressure to prove the return on marketing investments (ROMI). Customer advocacy marketing initiatives are no exception.

The cost of building a customer marketing program can be high, but companies definitely benefit in the long term. The benefit of increasing advocates for your brand, product, or service is great because the return is high: You are essentially getting free sales and marketing from those advocates. However, measuring that advocacy and reporting on ROMI is tricky business. It is nearly impossible to capture every element of customer advocacy and what customers advocated on your company's behalf. As difficult as the task is, CMOs who are eager to please their bosses must be able to discover what is measurable and report back that information. It is those bits and pieces of data that provide insights into your advocacy marketing effort's bottom line and give you an understanding of exactly what metrics moved the needle the most.

Jim Mooney, Dan Montoya, and Nichole Auston from RO Innovation shared their thoughts, expertise, and best practices on what, when, how, and why to measure for advocate marketing success. After doing this with best-in-class companies for over a decade, they have compiled the following best-practice metrics, which can help you prove advocate marketing's worth, along with their tips on avoiding some common mistakes surrounding their use and advice on taking it to the next level.

Measuring Advocate Marketing Is Vital But Hard

Regardless of a customer advocate marketing program's size or maturity, it can be easy for customer marketers to get caught up in the day-to-day tactical and operational tasks of their jobs:

- Producing new case studies for the sales team
- Fulfilling reference requests
- Lining up customer speakers for the next company event
- Pulling customer quotes for press releases
- Asking customers to share new content via social media
- Launching a new referral campaign

Being proactive with strategy and program improvement often gives way when customer marketing managers are continually stuck in the cycle of reactive tasks, thus program analysis and review of hard metrics often gets pushed to the back burner. But it is really important to ask some honest questions about your program:

- Is it aligned with corporate priorities?
- Is it aligned with key stakeholders, and the things they have charted you to do?
- Is it enabling the sales process to be more efficient and effective?
- Is it providing the greatest benefits possible to your customer advocates?
- Is it contributing to the company's revenue goals?
- Is it supporting key marketing initiatives and projects, like a new product launch?

CMOs must audit and analyze metrics of their advocate marketing program because they are charged with proving value of marketing investments. CEOs and boards of directors care about results and moving the needle. When they ask, "What was the return on investment in this program?" you don't want to be caught by surprise or be unprepared. Proving the investment in such a program comes down to showing measurable, quantitative, trackable results.

The good news is that 85 percent of B2B companies in a recent Demand Metric[1] survey are using some sort of metrics to track their customer marketing efforts. Measuring and reporting the results of your program helps you know which areas need more attention and focus, and which areas are thriving. It also helps you to do the following:

- Prove value and business impact
- Prove program improvement and growth
- Secure or increase program budget
- Secure or increase executive support

The bottom line is that without measurements, it is much harder to definitively prove your efforts are yielding the desired results on the company's bottom line.

That said, auditing a customer marketing program is not always a walk in the park either. It is one thing to ask the question, "What kind of results did we deliver?" It is another to determine the answer. Some key challenges to customer marketing program measurement are as follows:

- **Knowing when to measure**—The time and money you invest today will have an uncertain impact at an uncertain point in the future. Last month's video case study might deliver results next month or perhaps not for two years, but customer marketing managers need to decide where to invest their energy and budget today.

- **Multiple touches**—Various studies show at least seven or more marketing touches are needed to convert a cold lead into a sale. This confirms what every marketer knows: It takes multiple touches to create a customer. This makes it difficult to allocate revenue to any specific advocacy touch.

- **Multiple influencers**—The average buying committee at a midsized company comprises six people. In the case of larger companies or more complex purchases, such a committee can involve 21 or more influencers. Different marketing programs affect each individual differently, so it is a challenge to know which programs have the most impact.

- **Extraneous variables**—In many cases, factors outside marketing's control can significantly impact program results—from macroeconomic trends, to the weather, to the quality of the sales reps. If revenues increased because the economy improved, can marketers claim their programs delivered better return on investment (ROI)?

What You Should Measure

Like most marketing programs, advocate marketing should be measured and optimized over time. As part of this effort, marketing should analyze strategic metrics that show performance against business objectives like advocate revenue contribution. At the same time, marketing needs to pay attention to operational and tactical metrics that highlight things like advocate participation rates.

So which advocacy marketing metrics provide the most value? The answer depends on the goals of your organization.

Program Goals

What are your customer marketing objectives? Generate sales, expand brand awareness, increase revenues, enhance customer loyalty, improve customer experience, or something else? The dynamics, drivers, and priorities for a customer advocacy program are very different for every company. As such, you're going to set your own goals and measure against them.

RO Innovation has worked with companies of all sizes for over a decade on goals and processes for specifically making their customer reference programs thrive. Here are some examples of basic metrics to track achievement of reference program goals over a designated time period, whether annually, quarterly, monthly, or weekly.

Customer Reference Pipeline

- Number of new reference companies and contacts added to the program
- Number of nominations converted to references
- Reference customer scorecard tracking
- Gap analysis; reference pool versus number of requests

Request Fulfillment

- Number of requests fulfilled
- Request fulfillment time versus service level agreement (SLA)
- Requester feedback on reference experiences

Reference Asset Utilization and Development

- Number of internal team member downloads (assets and asset types)

- Number of external views (by prospects and customers)
- Number and status of assets in development process
- Number of assets produced

Let's look at the different types of metrics that when captured, analyzed, and used, give you a full view of the state, value, and potential of your program. These types are strategic, operational, and tactical.

Strategic Metrics: ROI and Business Impact

Strategic metrics should correlate with the larger goals of the program or organization as a whole. Most often, we see strategic metrics focused on measuring business impact. After all, the core of assessing and evaluating your program is ultimately to find out what impact it is having on revenue and ROI. Although it is easy to think about this and understand the nature and importance of it, only 36 percent of companies can accurately measure the ROI of their customer reference programs. That means for every 10 programs, 6 or 7 cannot tell you their value to the business—scary!

Demand Metric reports over 90 percent of B2B organizations have some sort of customer marketing efforts or function, and 53 percent of them report getting moderate to significant revenue as a result. The metrics most associated with moderate to significant revenue impact from customer marketing are "renewal rate or churn" (44 percent) and "customer influenced revenue via referrals or references" (42 percent). In fact, best-in-class companies that report higher revenue contribution rates from their customer marketing programs use "renewal rate or churn" as a metric 59 percent of the time and "customer influenced revenue via referrals or references" 53 percent of the time, compared with just 27 percent and 30 percent, respectively, for companies that report lower revenue impact.

The following sections describe some examples of ways you can measure the strategic business impact of customer advocacy programs.

Customer Renewal and Upsell Rates

Engaged, happy customers will renew and purchase additional products from you, so track renewal and upsell rates for advocates versus nonadvocate customers.

Lead Generation

Peer-referred leads are typically the highest converting B2B lead source. Referral leads typically convert at a rate of 4 to 10 times higher than leads from other sources. Track the number of leads generated by advocates, the percentage of them that convert to new customers, and the average value of advocate-referred deals. Comparing those with the same metrics for nonadvocate referred leads can make this metric stand out even more as a measurement of success.

Cost Per Acquisition

If you are able to identify the number of advocates your program generated, you can also measure the cost per acquisition (CPA) of those advocates. Was the cost of campaigning and recruiting them to your program above or below the plan? How long did it take? Is there room for improvement?

Impact on Closed Business

At best, only one third of companies track deals where references are supplied, so this is critical. However, formal technology platforms that integrate with CRM systems give CMOs a formal way to track reference activity against generated revenue. Measure the total dollar value of deals won by month or quarter, and references (both content assets and live activities) that were provided to assist in closing those deals. Measure the use of references in the following ways through the sales cycle:

- References listed in request for proposal (RFP) responses
- Live reference events supported
- Case studies, videos, and other content that leverage the voice of the customer

Recognizing that reference activity and reference assets are only a component of successful sales cycles, many companies actually ask their customers why their business was won. Often, the reply is "Because you were able to share references with us."

Return on Investment

Some reference programs measure the cost (infrastructure and staffing) to run their program against the value of deals won to assess the program's contribution to the business. Let's walk through an example for a SaaS-based software company.

There are four variables you will need to know:

- **Average gross sales value**—This may refer to the amount the customer spent on license fees. In this example, the average deal involving customer advocacy results in $75,000 revenue. Also assume the average tenure of a customer is five years. Thus, each customer is worth about $375,000 in gross revenues to the company.
- **Average cost per acquisition**—Let us assume the company spends $12,500 on average in sales and marketing to acquire each new customer.
- **Total external program costs**—This includes the advocacy solution provider technology and services, agency services to produce customer advocate assets, and so on. In this example, the SaaS company spends about $75,000 a year on external costs.

- **Total internal program costs**—This is staff costs for advocate program management, promotional costs related to the program, and so on. In this example, the company spent $100,000 this year.

Now plug them into this formula, and the benefits become obvious and data-verified (Figure 18.1).

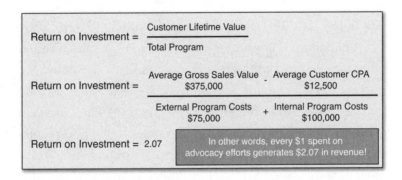

Figure 18.1 Calculating the return on investment for business impact

Sales Cycle Acceleration

Measure the length of sales cycles for deals that include customer reference participation and those that do not.

Asset Utilization

Measure what assets and asset types are used the most and consumed the most in sales cycles. Analytics can be run on several variables of the sales cycle, including industry, product, or geography. For example, analysis of which assets are viewed by prospects may indicate that case studies are consumed more by companies in manufacturing, and video testimonials are more interesting to companies in technology. This analysis helps marketing and content development teams prioritize and allocate their content budgets more effectively.

Operational Metrics: User Adoption and Stakeholder Awareness

Operational metrics track the performance of the advocate marketing program itself. The following sections list some examples of operation metrics to track.

Program Awareness

Avoid falling into the trap of thinking, "If you build it, they will come." It is important that your key stakeholders from sales, marketing, channel programs, and the customer community are inundated with programs, systems, tools, and processes to help them do their jobs. Thus, sometimes they forget your advocacy program is even out there. The reality is that your advocacy program is going to require announcement, promotions, reminders, and ongoing nurturing. Track login rates to your advocacy platforms, the stakeholder groups that use it most and least frequently, patterns in reference request rates, and responses on feedback surveys about your program.

Ease of Use

This is a qualitative metric that should not be overlooked. If you are not making your advocacy marketing program easy for your internal sales and marketing teams to use (including the platforms you choose to support it), they will not use it. It also means you are not likely to see the return on investment you desire. You can get a good reading on usability by surveying or interviewing your top users to get their opinions. From their candid feedback, figure out ways to make it even easier for them to use and get value to your program. Areas to measure include steps and time it took to find the correct advocate or reference asset, number of questions the team has about platform features, and so on.

Companies that are growing and nurturing user adoption typically do the following:

- Send frequent communications, announcements, and newsletters about their program to stakeholders.
- Leverage social media tools like Twitter and Chatter with stakeholders.
- Provide regular and frequent training sessions on how to leverage and use their program, platform, etc.
- Share stories of their peer's success using the advocacy program.

Customer Participation Rates

Obviously, a customer advocacy program provides no value unless you have a number of customer participants to call upon for requests. You should be measuring the percentage of your customer base willing to participate in some form of advocacy activity—and if that number is growing or shrinking. Look at net new advocates and slice by type, industry, solution, geography, and so on. This keeps your program fresh and adds to the currency and variety of advocates you can call upon to prevent reference fatigue or burnout.

Also remember that some customers only participate in your advocacy program for a limited time. They may leave the company or become dissatisfied and grumpy. Therefore, it is important to track ongoing engagement with metrics like number of responses per advocate and the number of advocates per campaign. Be sure to track the conversion rate for responses to asks, and determine participation distribution across the advocate pool.

User Adoption

Track the number of logins to your advocacy technology platforms, the number of new user logins, the number of support line requests, and feedback or ratings on program awareness surveys. These growth rates should be measured consistently over time.

It is also important to track exactly who is using your program and who your main stakeholders are (and if these are changing over time). You may have initially designed your program thinking sales would be the main users, but then find out that the marketing department uses it three times as much. This helps you position your program's assets and functionality to be useful and quickly adopted by the main user groups. It also helps you flag any areas or groups that you may need to readdress to increase user adoption.

Tactical Metrics: Asset Growth

These are the assets produced as a result of your advocates' labors. They should be tracked and analyzed against your objectives and compared monthly, quarterly, and annually. Some tactical metrics to track include those listed in the following sections.

Net New Assets

Look at the number of new customer reference and advocacy "assets" you can leverage in sales and marketing activities, such as case studies, reviews, quotes, testimonials, online reviews, and so on.

Reference Pool Growth

It is important to not only look at the total number of new advocates you are adding to your program, but to also look at new advocates by different categories (such as geography, solution/product, industry, activity, etc.). This ensures you have a well-rounded pool to call upon to prevent overuse of any one advocate, and also helps you flag any gaps that exist.

Advocacy Demand

This metric not only showcases the need for your program, but also its relevancy. Look at the types and frequency of advocates being requested for sales and marketing activities. This helps you see what types of advocates are most popular and what you need the most of, as well as discover where your program may be a little weak. Also look at the rate of fulfilled versus unfulfilled reference requests to determine if your reference database is current and on point enough to ensure you can fulfill current and future requests.

How Frequently Should We Measure?

Some metrics require continuous monitoring and data capture. Others require more periodic review, such as on a monthly or quarterly basis. Regardless, you should have the tools in place that allow you to constantly talk to your end-user base, to survey them, and to get their feedback. How you proceed depends on the types of metrics you are gathering and the interactions you are having.

Pitfalls and Advice

Although it's great to have key performance indicators (KPI) and metrics, it's also important to not get in over your head. Know where the KPI land mines are and how to avoid them:

- **Measuring without a goal in mind**—One of the most common mistakes we see in companies taking metrics is *not* measuring against goals. What we mean by that is they just jump right in. "We need to start a recruiting program" or "We need to go out and get nominations" without a target or goal in mind. As a result, their efforts and messaging are not very focused and they have nothing to measure against that would define success or failure for a KPI.

- **Not answering the "so what?"**—Another mistake is "measuring" basic numbers. "We've got 15 references in financial services, 10 in Product A, 17 for North America, 30 case studies, etc." The response is always, "so what?" It's good to know how many you have, but it is more important to know how many you need in each of those areas. Again, it goes back to the gap analysis mentioned earlier. Remember, it's not just about measuring activity, it's about measuring effectiveness.

- **Focusing only on financial**—It's not all about money. Not all KPIs need to be (or should be) financial. There are many qualitative metrics that help determine impact and success of a reference program.

- **Having too many KPIs**—Avoid "paralysis by analysis." Again, consider your organization's major goals and initiatives. If you really only need to track a handful of metrics, do it! Every company and program is different, so sometimes it's best to keep it simple!

- **Having hidden KPIs**—Once you have some solid data in your hands, don't keep it to yourself! Make sure you put your reports in the hands of those who need it. Because what good is a KPI if it's a secret?

Celebrate Your Program Along the Way

In addition to making a formal presentation and report package for your stakeholders, be sure to make the information dynamic. Alert the company when your program hits major milestones or goals. Invite yourselves to weekly sales team meetings. Get on their agenda.

Keep them aware of what's going on in your program. Ensure they know the benefits your program provides and the ways you can help them. That will go a long way in keeping your program successful and dynamic, and help aid the culture of customer-centricity you aim to support.

Let Metrics Serve as the Guardrails for Future Decisions

Through the process of assessing, measuring, and validating their program in a formal, organized way, CMOs are able to leverage the information it produces to let it guide future decisions in regard to the following:

- Budgets
- Staffing
- Asset development
- Advocate recruiting targets
- Customer reference fulfillment targets
- Business processes
- Technology platforms
- Executive support

Conclusion

When it comes to verifying and assessing how KPIs are met and tracking the ROI of your customer reference management program to executive management, identifying and capturing the right data, then constantly reporting on and promoting your program's progress is the key. A disciplined approach to reporting your program's performance, coupled with presenting the information in meaningful, easy-to-digest indicators for the executive team, means that you will not only strengthen your customer marketing program year over year, but you will also increase your budgets with amplified executive support.

Highlights and Takeaways

The following are a few highlights and takeaways from this chapter:

- Measuring and reporting the results of your program helps you know what areas need more attention and focus.
- Measuring and analyzing data points helps ensure buy-in from decision makers.
- Understand and know your customer marketing objectives.
- Strategic metrics should correlate with the larger goals of the program or organization as a whole.
- Avoid paralysis by analysis. If you really only need to track a handful of metrics, do it.

About Nichole Auston

Nichole Auston is the marketing director at RO Innovation. She has honed expertise in online content development, sales enablement, customer advocate marketing, SMB Internet marketing strategy, e-mail marketing, pay-per-click advertising, and social media outreach. Her "can do" attitude and a passion for the results produced both online and offline drives success at RO Innovation.

Auston's marketing experience covers a variety of fast-paced industries, including software, health care, financial services, industrial manufacturing, travel, real estate, career services, and more. Before coming on board at RO Innovation, she worked in marketing capacities at Access Marketing Company, Republic Financial, 90Octane, University of Denver, and Shea Properties.

Auston has a bachelor of science in business administration in marketing with a minor in real estate from the Daniels College of Business at the University of Denver.

About Jim Mooney

Jim Mooney is the founder and CEO of RO Innovation. He is a seasoned business professional with an extensive background in all levels of sales and business development. With over 30 years of professional experience, Mooney has worked in and with major companies in several industries, including high-tech and enterprise software.

Prior to founding RO Innovation, Mooney served as vice president of North American sales for Deuxo, Inc., where he brought the company to a new level of prosperity. Throughout his career, he has found success at all levels of sales, including the selling of complex business solutions to large corporations, such as Coca-Cola, American Airlines, Walmart, United Airlines, and Shell.

In 2002, after seeing a need for a sales technology in the marketplace that could deliver optimized sales tools and customer reference assets to prospects and provide intelligence on when and what tools the prospect engaged with, he founded RO Innovation. In his current role as CEO, Mooney has strategically guided the company to be a true innovator and pioneer in sales and marketing technology. He has been instrumental in the development and evolution of the company's customer reference management platform and enterprise-level sales enablement solution, and is always seeking new ways RO

Innovation can help enterprises make sales easier, close rates faster, foster better customer relationships, and create integrated solutions.

Mooney holds a bachelor of science degree in business from Fort Lauderdale College.

About Dan Montoya

Dan Montoya is the vice president of professional services at RO Innovation. He is a customer-oriented business professional with over 25 years of combined experience in consultative sales, marketing, business process consulting, and program and operations management.

Montoya has worked directly with major companies in several industries, including high-tech, enterprise software, aerospace, industrial, energy, medical, pharmaceutical, and consumer goods. Prior to joining RO Innovation, he was the program manager of consulting services for i2 Technologies where he was responsible for successful customer implementations of supply chain management solutions and generation of $5 million in annual services revenue.

Other assignments include presales business consulting at i2 where he contributed to over $10 million in annual sales; knowledge management where he was responsible for development and delivery of training, coaching, and materials for i2 presales consultants; and product marketing for SMC Networks, where he developed marketing programs to support generation of $30 million in annual revenue. Montoya was also the director of professional services for CADIS, a component and supplier management solutions company where he established the services practice and organization, responsible for successful customer implementations and generation of over $3 million.

Dan holds a bachelor of science degree in natural resources management from Colorado State University and a master of business administration from the University of Phoenix.

Nichole, Jim, and Dan Are Advocates

Nichole is an advocate of Shaklee cleaning products because they are green, safe, smart, and powerful. They are made with nontoxic, ecofriendly ingredients (more so than any "green" cleaner found at stores) and are better than the "green" "make it yourself" versions found on Pinterest or the Web. Plus, their packaging is biodegradable and uses less materials than conventional cleaners. Shaklee says their Starter Kit can save users $3,400 on equivalent cleaners, can eliminate 108 pounds of packaging waste from landfills, and can keep 248 pounds of greenhouse gasses out of the atmosphere. Because Shaklee products don't contain nasty chemicals or fumes, Nichole has peace of mind knowing she is not exposing her small children to dangerous chemicals, especially if they were to get their hands on them and do some "cleaning" of their own. Because Shaklee's cleaning products are sold as a concentrate, it is cheaper for Nichole and lasts her longer. She can also clean in more ways based on the dilution she uses. "Seriously, a little goes a long way with this stuff and always gets the job done in no time at all...it's awesome! You wouldn't believe some of the before and after photos I've taken simply because my friends didn't believe the power of this stuff!" she says.

Jim Mooney is an advocate of Office Evolutions, an office space provider for small businesses throughout the United States. As a busy CEO and salesperson, Mooney loves the flexibility and convenience of being able to reserve a professional office or meeting space in the major cities where he travels. He also notes that the staff at Office Evolution is always extremely accommodating and always goes out of their way. "Whether I need a conference room or meeting space at the last minute, or need them to run something to the mail for me at 5:00 p.m., they've always been super accommodating and helpful with any request I have. As such, I end up recommending them to my business friends all the time!"

Dan Montoya is an advocate of TaylorMade golf clubs. He likes the quality of their products and variety of their club choices. He also likes that they continue to offer new products regularly with the latest golf technology. "I have never had a bad experience with their product...other than my own golf swing!" Montoya says.

Endnote

1. Demand Metric, Customer Marketing Benchmark Report, September 2014, http://www.demandmetric.com/content/customer-marketing-benchmark-report.

19

Epilogue: What's Next?
Using What You Have Learned

At this point, you have heard from the experts. So the next logical question is, "What does this mean for me? What can I do with this information to build a terrific advocate marketing program for my organization?"

The road map in this chapter pulls together the wisdom of the experts in a way that gives you, the professional, solid direction to build such a program. This list is not exhaustive, but using your own creativity, this guidance can be fine-tuned to fit your organization. Don't forget, the experts are also mentors and are available for consultation and advice; their contact information is the "Interviewees' Contact Information" chapter near the end of this book.

1. Identify the activities that are valuable to you and your organization. For example, you may need several customers to provide testimonials or case studies. On the other hand, you might need to produce three webinars that include customers, or you might need five customers to participate in speaking engagements. You'll include these types of activities in your survey. Determine a score for each of these activities. As an example, a testimonial earns 5 points, a webinar earns 15 points, but a speaking engagement earns 25 points.

2. Consult your corporate attorneys to develop a release form for customers to sign that gives permission for public use of their company's name and logo on advocates' testimonials.

3. Build the customer engagement survey. Include the five basic questions that the customers will complete (listed below). When you build the survey (using an online survey tool), remember that each question leads to the next based on the customer's response. You may want to include a text box on the survey so that customers who (for example) indicate that they will provide a testimonial can immediately do so. When finished, the survey results help you assess their willingness to engage in the different activities. The questions include:

    a. How satisfied are you?

    b. Are you willing to recommend?

    c. Would you be a reference?

    d. Are you willing to engage?

    e. Which of these activities would you be willing to do? (sample activities)

        i. Provide a testimonial

        ii. Speak at a webinar

        iii. Speak at an event

        iv. Provide a case study

4. Contact all of your customers. Send them a link to your customer engagement survey.

5. Identify a tool—a spreadsheet, a database, etc.—that you will use to track and manage the results. Using software, rather than pen and paper, makes tracking and analyzing the responses and results much more manageable, less prone to human error and bias, and allows you to objectively analyze the results to make good determinations. An online tool also saves you a huge amount of time and gives much more flexibility and mobility. The contributors to this book have made several suggestions for reliable online tools, and they can be contacted for further advice.

6. Assess and qualify your advocates.

    a. Perform the survey. Customers take the customer engagement survey.

    b. Identify your advocates who score 9 and 10. To do so, categorize the customers based on the activities they are willing to perform. An automated tool may do this for you.

    c. Assess the results. Group the results by the following:

        i. Viability as an advocate

        ii. Geographic location

        iii. Activities they're willing to perform

7. Put your advocates to work. Lock in their commitment and date to accomplish the activities they've agreed to. For example, for the customers who agree to write a testimonial, ask them to give you that testimonial right on the survey. For the customers who agree to participate in webinars, set up a date, time, and subject (e.g., the implementation of your product, the experience of implementation, the successful results of the implementation, etc.).

8. Once customers have performed the activity, you or your employees log that the activity has been completed. This can be done in a spreadsheet or software. At this point, points are assigned to the advocate based on the assigned value of the activity. For the organization, the score denotes the value of each advocate to the organization. The advocate also benefits by increased influence and esteem as a thought leader in the industry.

9. Leverage the activity. For example, if an advocate has written a case study, identify and use the pieces within the case study (or group components with other content pieces) to create content for social media, new collateral, testimonial for Web sites, webinars, speaking events, and the like.

10. Thank the advocates through public acknowledgment of their achievements just as they have publicly shared their success with you.

11. Evaluate and analyze the impact of the advocates and their activities. Key performance indicators include (but are not limited to):

    a. The influence advocate marketing has on a sale. Don't forget that third-party endorsements have much more influence on sales than any endorsements that come from within the organization itself. Advocates help shorten the timeline of a sale.

    b. Whether a customer reference was involved in the sales process, and did that sale close as a win or a loss. This helps to tie the advocate's work to revenue.

    c. Quantify the amount of press (including social media buzz, press releases, and the like) the organization gets from the content created by the advocate.

    d. Evaluate the prestige of the advocate. For example, what percentage of Fortune 500 companies or Dow Jones Sustainable Index companies can you include as advocates? Endorsement by such respected organizations enhances your third-party validation, positive relevance, and brand recognition.

    e. Identify the geographic distribution of your advocates to know who they are, where they are, and what they will do to help you determine where more focus is needed, where you can expect greater return, and where there are opportunities to grow.

    f. Evaluate your organization's products and business lines in terms of which have more advocates than others.

12. Let your organization know just who your real advocates are based on their successful completion of engagement, and how they benefit the organization. This is information to be broadcast, not kept sequestered in the advocacy marketing program's team and database. This is a key point in an organization's goal to keep the customer first. Let the world know that your customer advocates love you. In other words, advocate for your advocates.

To sustain your program, repeat these steps. Reexamine your policies. Reevaluate your advocates (an advocate today might not be your advocate tomorrow). Review the engagement activities that are important to your organization that only an advocate can perform. In other words, like your advocates, your advocate marketing program requires nurturing and attention.

Interviewees' Contact Information

Nichole Auston
Marketing Director
1624 Market Street, Suite 202
Denver, CO 80202
nauston@roinnovation.com
Phone: 888.731.4002 x 706
Cell: 303.241.4451

Greg Coticchia
Director, "The Blast Furnace" Student Accelerator, University of Pittsburgh
CEO, ENTRA Inc.
246 Cedar Boulevard
Pittsburgh, PA 15228
gcoticchia@innovation.pitt.edu
greg@entrainc.com
Phone: 412.401.5423
Twitter: @GregCott

Lawrence D. Dietz
General Counsel and Managing Director, Information Security
TAL Global Corporation
1 Almaden Blvd., Suite 750
San Jose, CA 95113
ldietz@talglobal.net
Phone: 408.993.1300

Brian Gladstein
briangladstein@gmail.com
Twitter: @briangladstein

Neil Hartley
https://www.linkedin.com/in/neilhartley

Reid Hawkins
3608 Summer Leaf Ct.
Raleigh, NC 27615
reidhawkins@nc.rr.com
Phone: 919.841.1555
Cell: 919.349.9399

Evan Jacobs
https://www.linkedin.com/in/evanjacobsprofile
Twitter: @EvanJ2011

Scott Jaworski
www.linkedin.com/in/scottjaworski
Twitter: @scott_jaworski

Pamela Kiecker Royall, PhD
Head of Research
Royall & Company
pkiecker@royall.com
Phone: 804.741.6337 x 1254

Sandra Lopez
https://www.linkedin.com/in/lopezsandra
Twitter: @NYCSF

Dan Montoya
Vice President of Professional Services
1624 Market Street, Suite 202
Denver, CO 80202
dmontoya@roinnovation.com

Jim Mooney
Chief Executive Officer
1624 Market Street, Suite 202
Denver, CO 80202
jmooney@roinnovation.com

Lee Rubin
Senior Manager, Global Reference Programs
Citrix Systems, Inc.
lee.rubin@citrix.com

Sylvia E. Salazar-Botero
https://www.linkedin.com/in/sylviaesalazar
Twitter: @theGeekyBird

Barbara Thomas, CDM, CeM
Creative Tactics, LLC
bt@creativetactics.com
Phone: 301.728.2503
Twitter: @creativetactics
LinkedIn: www.linkedin.com/in/barbaraannthomas

Jim Williams
Vice President of Marketing
Influitive
Phone: 781.718.1435
Twitter: @jimcwilliams, @influitive

Steven Wyer
Phone: 615.224.6610
Twitter: swyer@3Ci.agency

Index

C

growth, asset, 184-185
Gruehl, Douglas, 130-131, 134
guest blogging, 75
GYK Antler, 22, 62

H-I

Hartley, Neil, 100, 105
Harvard Business School, 145
Hawkins, Reid, 107, 114
Heuer, Megan, 165
identities, online, 149-150
incentives, promotions, 113
Incubatus, LLC, 100. *See also*
  Hartley, Neil
*Industrial Safety & Hygiene
  News*, 48
influencers, 8, 57
Influitive, 22, 117
Infographic Journal, 9
Information Operations and
  Psychological Operations
  (PSYOP), 133
infrastructures, marketing, 92-94
Institute of Public Relations, 62
Intel, 22
  advocate marketing, 84-85
  product launches, 79
  Smart Squad teams, 82-84
internal audit and infrastructure
  stage, 159-160
internal metrics, 68
internal program costs, 181
internal team organization, 5
interviews, 41-44
Intuit, 14
Iron Mountain, 14

J-K

Jacobs, Evan, 71-72, 74, 76-77
Jaworski, Scott, 79-82, 88-89. *See
  also* Smart Squad teams

key performance indicators (KPIs),
  31, 185-186
Klout scores, 19, 58
Kodak, 14

L

leadership. *See also* management
  do as I say, not as I do, 127
  top-down internal advocate
    cultures, 66-67
lead generation, 179
LinkedIn, 4, 85, 149
listening skills, 21
Lopez, Sandra, 79-82, 87-88. *See
  also* Smart Squad teams
loyalty, customers, 62

M

management
  Advocate Recognition
    Engagement (ARE)
    programs, 155-159
  crisis, 45
  do as I say, not as I do, 127
  measuring, 68-69
  references, 100-102
  reputation, 143. *See also*
    reputation management
  top-down internal advocate
    cultures, 66-67
margins, 111
Maritz Research, 145
marketing
  achievements, 82-84
  auditing, 175
  automation, 101
  budgets, 14
  disruptive, 123
  importance of, 13-14
  infrastructures, 92-94